T5-AFZ-318

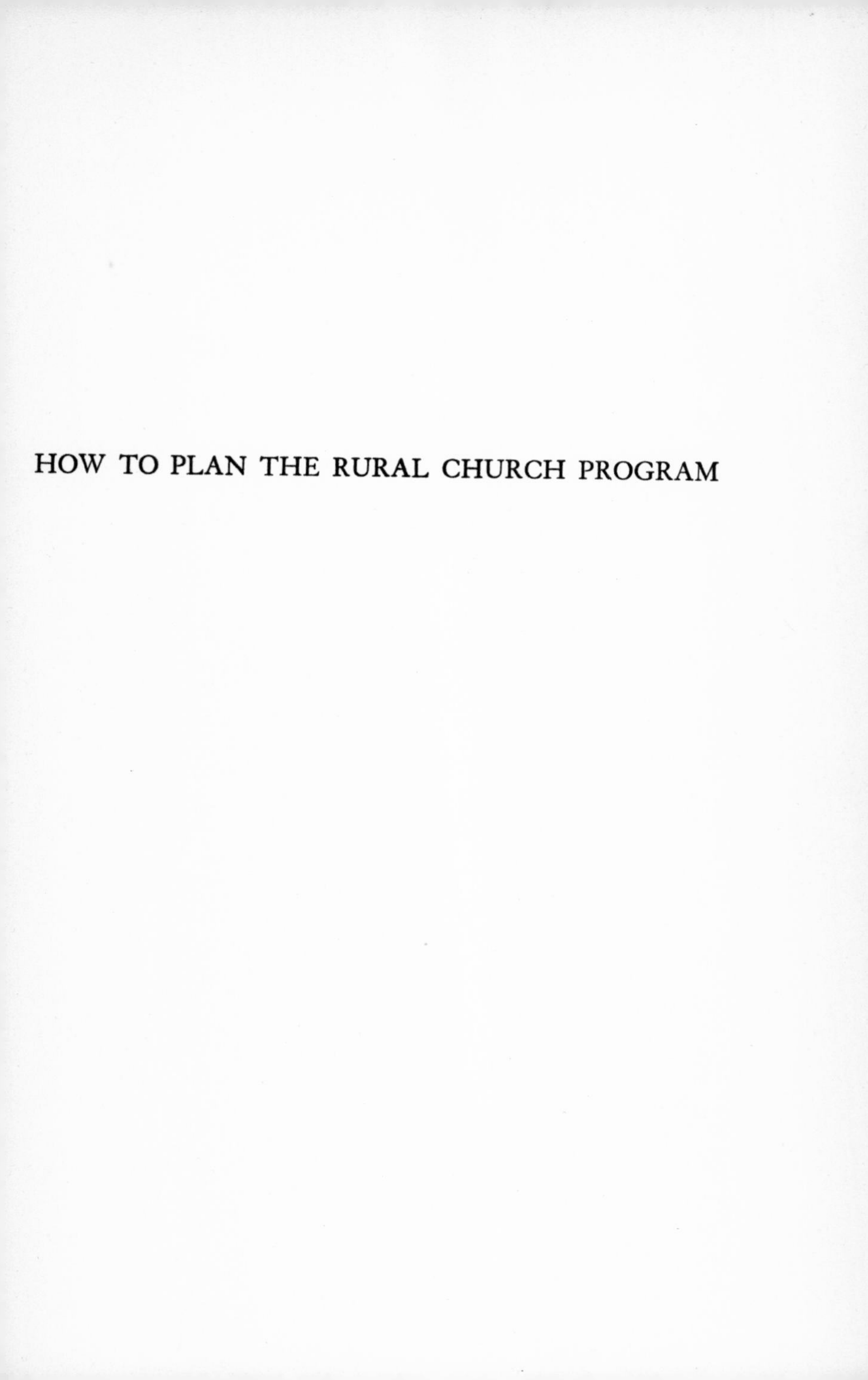

HOW TO PLAN THE RURAL CHURCH PROGRAM

How to Plan the Rural Church Program

by

CALVIN SCHNUCKER

Philadelphia

THE WESTMINSTER PRESS

Library of Congress Catalog Card Number: 54-5281

PRINTED IN THE UNITED STATES OF AMERICA

CONTENTS

Foreword 7

Part One

SEARCHING FOR FACTS

1. Introduction and Retrospect 11
2. Studies in Community 19
3. Studies in Family 31
4. Studies in the Local Church 40

Part Two

BUILDING THE PROGRAM

5. Analyzing and Interpreting the Steps 57
6. Setting Up Goals 72
7. Developing the Program and Checking Results 82

Part Three

EXTENDING THE PROGRAM

8. The Unreached 97
9. The Denominational Parish 109
10. The Interdenominational Parish 121
11. The Difficult Parish 129
12. Financing the Rural Church 137
13. The Rural Church Building 148
14. The Forward Look 153

Bibliography 157

FOREWORD

ALL MY MEMORIES, both from boyhood days and from recent years, are centered in the rural church. No matter in which state I traveled, always I found the rural church. With its people I have worshiped in Vermont and New York, in South Dakota and Montana, in Arkansas and Kentucky. For five years I served them as a public-school teacher. During that time some of their problems became apparent. However, it was during the ten years when I served as pastor of an open country church in Iowa that the amazing changes in rural living with their attendant problems really troubled me. After I had studied these changes and problems for another decade, this book resulted.

It is a book for rural church leaders, especially those who are concerned about the church and its problems and who are casting about for simple aids to assist them in developing more adequate plans for their local churches.

It is a book for students who plan to enter the service of the rural church. For them it seeks to open the doors to a fuller understanding of the problems, the solutions to those problems, and the challenge of the rural area.

In an attempt to make this book readable, footnotes and technical data have been omitted. A bibliography has been included, with a statement about each suggested piece of material.

For help and inspiration I am greatly indebted to my many friends who have given their lives to rural work: Dr. W. H. Stacy and Dr. Ray Wakely, of Iowa State College; Dr. John H. Kolb, of the University of Wisconsin; Dr. C. Morton Hanna, of Louisville Presbyterian Seminary.

This book is dedicated to my wife, Wilhelmine, and my daughters, Florence and Joyce, who chose to live the simple rural life with me in preference to the city and were of constant encouragement while this book was prepared.

CALVIN SCHNUCKER.

Part One

SEARCHING FOR FACTS

Chapter 1

INTRODUCTION AND RETROSPECT

As COMMON as death and taxes, yet much more apparent, are the churches. Whether one drives through county seat towns, through the flat and wealthy corn land, or across meadows and hills, they are there. Just around the bend, or on the side of the hill, or four strong in the village, the rural churches stand. Some are barren, gloomy, and full of decay; others are white, well-kept spires pointing Godward, full of the promise of life. These are the churches that teamed together with our forefathers to make America strong. Education, culture, spiritual development, altruism, all owe their nineteenth century impetus to these early-founded churches.

Though they played a magnificent part in the early history of our land, they seemed unable to adjust themselves to the rapid changes that were taking place in late nineteenth and early twentieth century American life. The schools adjusted themselves to the needs of the people, businesses soon found their existence level, but the churches which once had flourished began to die.

The roots of the American rural church problem are not to be found in the United States. Rather are they to be found in the spires, the great organs, the stained-glass windows, and the heavy rock walls of the European cathedrals. Christianity, as it developed after the Roman Empire made it the official State religion, has always been urban-centered. The masses of population were town- and city-centered. It seemed most appropriate to build the cathedral type of church where the densest population was located. Consequently, urban concepts of church work always prevailed in Europe.

The rural people who desired to attend services would walk to the nearest town or city. They had little to say concerning the development of church life. Most of the working class among the farmers did not attend the church services. Religion to them became an obligation of the family. The landowner did take a fairly active part in the urban church life because he had his horses and carriage for transportation. The peasants (cotters in England), although they seldom attended the worship service, took on the same form of sectarian Christianity that was held by the landlord. The over-all consequence of this system was that Christianity in Europe became an urban, cathedral-centered concept.

With immigration to the United States came the same church concepts that were long held by the European nationals, with one exception: the idea of separation of Church and State early took root here. More and more immigrants arrived on our shores; they pressed ever farther inland. Land was plentiful; it seemed inexhaustible. So long as expansion of population continued, the European concept of church seemed adequate. Each group of immigrants brought its particular brand of sectarian Christianity along and organized a church on that basis. If our country had developed the same density of population that plagued central Europe, a rural church problem would not have developed. However, as small numbers of Lutherans, Reformed, Roman Catholics, and Methodists moved into the same approximate neighborhood, each group sought to develop its own denominationalism. By the end of the nineteenth century it became apparent that the rural population would soon reach its greatest extension, and that the population density per square mile would fall far short of that in Europe. The result of this stabilization of population immediately reflected itself in church life and activity. Quite different from in Europe, there were not sufficient people in any given rural area to support all the denominations represented in the population. This was not so apparent at first while population was growing and goods rather than money was the medium of exchange.

With the adoption of the principle of separation of Church and State, Government support of churches did not long exist in the United States. Thus by 1915, without an adequate population density and without Government support, the churches serving the rural areas were in deep trouble. It has been exceedingly difficult to understand just why this trouble has developed and just how to overcome it. Because we have been unable to shake ourselves loose from the old European concepts of church, serious decay has struck deeply at the heart of the church.

There were men who realized what this decay in rural life would mean to the nation as a whole. Theodore Roosevelt, Warren Wilson, Dwight Sanderson, Liberty Hyde Bailey, and others became greatly concerned. Already fifty years ago these men began the long and arduous task of rebuilding rural America with its basic institutions. It was no easy task. People whose minds were engrossed with the materialistic advantages made possible in a period of advancing mechanization were not interested in what was happening to their own rural institutions.

Two major evils were making rapid headway in the lives of the people. Because of man's great interest in the advances toward wealth through mechanization, he ignored what he was doing to the soil which in the final analysis was the basic source of his wealth. Erosion began taking its toll. In what was once a lush southland, cotton and tobacco were robbing the soil of its fertility and caused this soil to erode and degenerate until it was all but valueless. In the Midwest the ax felled the trees on the hills and the plow cut deeply through the soil that had been cleared, until, with no cover to hold it, the earth was washed from the hillside, across the plains, down the river into the sea — forever lost. In the Great Plains region the wild grasses were turned under, and repeated plantings of wheat loosened the light loams until they became the prey of the wind and were blown across the continent far out to sea.

Concurrent with the evil of soil erosion, the degeneration of men's souls took place. The family began to disintegrate; the neighborhood lost its identity. Because the churches were no longer maintained, a period of spiritual decadence and deterioration developed which became manifest across the land. Church leaders became greatly concerned, sociologists recognized the trend and were burdened by it, educators took cognizance of the conditions. All recognized that a strong rural church held the key to the solution of these newly created problems.

From the time that men became aware of the special need in rural life, two periods of rural church work have developed. The first I have called "The Nostalgic Period"; the second, for want of a better name, "The Save Yourself Period."

The Nostalgic Period

This concept was developed around memories — memories of men who once lived, memories of experiences in childhood days glorified and almost deified by the passage of time. Men recalled the times when the rural church was the heart and center of almost every neighborhood and community. It was the social center. After services families would gather together and visit. Relatives who had no opportunity to see each other except at church would avidly visit for a while. Grandchildren would rush over to the grandparents and tell them about the new kittens or the little lamb that had to be fed by bottle. It was not unusual to see people standing around the church an hour after the services had ended.

The rural church was the recreational center. The author well remembers the "singing school" held on Wednesday evenings. Young men with their spirited horses and fancy harnesses would meet at the mile corner north of church and the mile corner south of church. Then the races would begin. Madly galloping horses, bouncing buggies, and screaming sisters would finally come to a halt in the shelter barns across the road from the church. Many of the best horse races that ever took place in Stephenson County, Illinois, were held just before singing school.

It was the best matrimonial agency. No dance halls, no moving picture theaters, no roller skating rinks, no drive-ins — only the church was available. So, during the preaching of the long and somewhat dry sermon — in fact, furtively even during the impassioned prayer — the young made eyes at each other from behind the open pages of the hymnal. A coveted nod from the brown-eyed brunette meant a date after Wednesday night's singing school. A negative shake of the head saddened the heart of many an ardent swain.

It was the spiritual center, where confessions of faith came with conviction. It was no easy matter to stand up before a congregation to be questioned by the elders of the church. Especially was this true when the other young folks in the gallery remembered the joint escapade of only a month ago. These buddies had to be faced later. There would be a great deal of joshing and some rather trying insinuations. But in this early rural church faith and works were inseparable handmaidens.

Remembering this with nostalgia, the early rural church workers thought that if a few demonstration parishes were again set up, subsidized with denominational monies, others seeing would be glad to follow. Here and there, with conditions favorable, it was possible to reconstruct such a picture, but the fast-moving and changing twentieth century civilization could not be stopped. The rural church impetus of the early part of this century did little more than focus the attention of a subsequent generation upon the fact that a rural church problem existed. It was to church life what the bee and flower explanation of sex was to the moral edification of the same generation, namely, inadequate and merely curiosity-provoking.

Thereupon followed the depression, economically and spiritually devastating. Those early years of the thirties were so powerful in their influence that the attention that had been focused on the rural church was diverted to the problem of economic and political survival. Demonstration churches passed from the picture. But gradually, as a different economic pattern evolved, a new rural pattern developed. Born of the depression, the two had this one factor in common — they were both based upon the principle of stark survival.

The Save Yourself Period

This second concept or period I have dubbed "The Save Yourself Period." Totally un-Biblical, it developed more catch phrases and deafening statistics than had ever been conceived possible. The leaders told urban church men that they had better become interested in the rural church; otherwise their constant stream of transfer members would dry up. They said that most of the able leaders in every area of life today came from rural areas. This leadership was purported to be Christian — hence if they did not save the rural church, Christian leadership would die out. "Save the rural church" became a catch phrase. Appeals for funds were based upon the necessity of saving the rural church. Grudging denominational aid was forced by the dire forecast, " The bogeyman will get you if you don't save the rural church." In many cases that is where the so-called rural church program and problem finds itself now. Basically, the concept is one of selfishness. It is in keeping with man's mad chase after the elusive goal of personal security. As in other areas of life, a selfish concept can give an amazing lift and impetus toward a desired goal; even though the motive may be wrong, or at best ill-placed, the results can be quite amazing. So it has been during the past five or ten years. The results of this lift and the wide publicity and the decisive denominational action have been almost immeasurable. In spite of all this the rural church continues to decay, the community continues to dissipate, the family continues to disintegrate, and the social solidarity of the neighborhood continues to be liquidated. Thus always it will happen when an all-out effort is made to save one's self or one's institution for the sake of the self or the institution.

Thus today many realize that it is high time to do some re-evaluating and rethinking concerning rural church work. The real reasons that the earlier concepts of rural church rehabilitation did not succeed so adequately as was hoped are twofold. First, the concept and procedures were based at best on an only partially true premise. To strengthen or to save any institution either for nostalgic or for selfish reasons is bound to lead to failure. The second reason was that the earlier leaders had not taken into account the background philosophy and technique out of which American rural churches were born.

During the past twenty years rural sociologists have done the cause of town and country life a real service in carefully analyzing the conditions that were gradually leading to decay in most of the rural institutions. However, even among our sociologists the causes were sought in the actual change from a simple agrarian philosophy to a new mechanized materialist way of living. Some of the roots of decay are to be found in this changing process. But, as we have seen, the fundamental cause must be traced back much farther than the immediate past. Sociologists have pointed out what is happening, but have carefully avoided the development of lines of action whereby the trends could be changed.

In the following chapters the author proposes to approach the rural church problem with only one purpose in mind, namely, to point out an action program which, when followed, will help to meet the religious needs of rural people through an understanding and tailor-made church program. Old techniques and tools which have proved useful will be polished and brought up to date. Some new skills and methods will be presented which may not fit the governmental policy of all denominations but which ought nevertheless to have a fair trial. So that these skills and techniques may be presented most intelligently, the author finds it necessary to shift the emphasis from the church to the people. Most books on methods glorify the local church organization: how to increase the membership, how to organize a rousing good youth club, how to build and departmentalize the Sunday church school, how to develop finances in the church, how to create an efficient, ongoing, over-all church program. These concerns have occupied the pages of most technique books and have been the usual road of approach in the minds of church leaders.

In the pages that follow a different emphasis has been made. The church, though important in its function, has yielded the place of centrality to persons. People are of primary concern. How best can the church serve rural people? Through what avenue can the evangel of Christ be made most vital to people? These are the questions that must be answered. This does not mean that the church with its local organizations is incidental to the entire picture of service. It merely indicates that the church must be strong so that its people may be strong, that the church must be efficient so that the people may best be served, that the church must be effective so that people may best be reached. It is merely the indication of a change of emphasis.

The first part of this book deals with studies in the community, the family, and the local church. Techniques of analysis are presented that may be used by any rural pastor in his approach to a better understanding of the people he serves. The second portion directs the pastor in setting up goals, developing a program to fill the needs of his people, and a procedure by which he can check the results. The final portion of the book deals with lines of action that will be of greatest value in reaching and serving that part of our rural population which, because of either the decadence or the unimaginativeness of the rural church, remains uncontacted.

Chapter 2

STUDIES IN COMMUNITY

THE MINISTER who accepts the responsibility of ministering to a local church cannot assume that his service shall be delegated to that church alone. He must immediately take cognizance of the community as a part of which his church is functioning. To separate person from community is to give impetus to the fragmentation of society which at the present time is only too evident in rural America. One of the really tragic factors that has done much to dissipate the influence of the rural church has been the indifferent stubbornness of church leaders in ignoring the community and its relationship to people.

DEFINITION OF COMMUNITY

Whenever the community is discussed, it automatically becomes necessary to define just what is meant. There are almost as many definitions of the concept "community" as there are those who write about it. C. J. Galpin wrote in his book *The Social Anatomy of an Agricultural Community* (University of Wisconsin Research Bulletin No. 34, 1915, p. 18): "It is difficult, if not impossible, to avoid the conclusion that the trade zone about one of these rather complete agricultural civic centers forms the boundary of an actual, if not legal, community, within which the apparent entanglement of human life is resolved into a fairly unitary system of interrelatedness. The fundamental community is a composite of many expanding and contracting feature communities possessing the characteristic pulsating instability of all real life."

Lowry Nelson (in *Rural Sociology,* American Book Co., 1948, p. 75), defined the community thus: "In general, the term community refers to a group of people inhabiting a limited area, who have a sense of belonging together and who through their organized relationships share and carry on activities in pursuit of their common interests."

Dwight L. Sanderson (in *The Rural Community,* Ginn & Co., 1932, p. 481), whose definition has almost become the classical one acceptable to most rural sociologists, says, " It consists of the social interactions of the people and their institutions in the local area in which they live on dispersed farmsteads and in a hamlet or village which forms the center of their common activities." Others have described the community as a quality of solidarity, mutuality, and togetherness displayed by a group of people. Baker Brownell, in his recent book, *The Human Community* (Harper & Brothers, 1950), lists five characteristics of the community: " (1) A community is a group of neighbors who know one another face to face. (2) It is a diversified group as to age, sex, skill function, and mutual service to each other. (3) It is a co-operative group in which many of the main activities of life are carried on together. (4) It is a group having a sense of 'belonging' or group identity and solidarity. (5) It is a rather small group, such as the family, village, or small town, in which each person can know a number of others as whole persons, not as functional fragments. When the group under consideration is so large that the people in it do not know one another, the community disappears."

In objectively analyzing the many definitions that have been given for community it becomes apparent that community may mean many different things. (1) It may be geographic. Definite boundaries are recognizable which limit the services and activities to a certain area. Frequently these boundaries may be a chain of hills, a valley, a river, a state or county line, or any combination of these. (2) It may have its scope determined by the extent of services that are made possible by business and professional men living within its center. A community has developed around a small town. The doctor serves people in a circle approximately five miles out from the center. People drive in from an area of twenty-eight square miles to do their trading. The bank numbers its depositors from almost the same territory. The consolidated school and the churches also find the greatest part of their constituency within six miles of the village center. (3) It may even be philosophic, determined by the factors of mutuality, togetherness, understanding, and unity which have resulted from a group of people living in the same general area and knowing each other quite well.

So far as my use of the concept of community for this writing is concerned, a combination of all three of these factors must be considered. The effectiveness of the primary institutions functioning within the community can be no greater than either the deliberate or the unconscious consent of the members of the community permits it to be.

The above statement is especially pertinent to the work of the church, although it is not often recognized as a determining factor. Too often the local church carries on an interest program entirely outside of the community framework. As a result, the community suffers fragmentation at the hands of the one organization that ought to work for unity, solidarity, and oneness. A pastor who is thoroughly interested in the welfare of the people he serves will immediately recognize his need to familiarize himself with the structure of the community so that he with his church program may be most helpful to all. Because persons cannot, except in unusual circumstances, be isolated from community, it becomes mandatory for the church as an institution to strengthen the community.

Understanding the Community — Its History

The historic background of each individual American community is of marked significance. The usual community is still so near its source that any planning that is to be done must reckon with these sources. There are several historical factors that the pastor must carefully consider. Many communities originally developed because ethnic groups migrated from Europe and, wishing to retain many of their old customs and traditions, settled as a group, thus forming a community. Even after several generations have passed, a denomination foreign to the Old World experience of this group would find it difficult to develop a program among such people. For example, in northwest Iowa many communities developed around the immigrations of Dutch people. These folks brought with them from

Holland not only their customs and language but also their own pastors. They built strong churches in which the congregations for many years used the Dutch language. As years passed, other settlers moved into the territory; after several generations of intermarriage and migration there is a goodly minority of people who are not so closely related to the old Dutch Church and customs as others. Despite this, it would be difficult for a Methodist to attempt a mission in the community.

Many times a pastor who has had a degree of success in one church moves into another area which on the surface seems to present about the same challenge as the community did from which he moved. After much effort the pastor discovers that his work is not blessed with the same degree of success as formerly. He might have discovered this even before contemplating the move if he had carefully investigated the history of the development of the community to which he proposed moving. A pastor who is interested in making the greatest contribution to the life of his community needs, therefore, carefully to assess the history and background of the people in his area.

The sources of information are not always readily available. In almost every community, however, they may be found after expending some effort. There is, first of all, the public library. In many rural areas the nearest public library is located in the county seat town. A trip to this library will be very rewarding. During the depression the Government, through subsidies set up through the WPA, engaged unemployed people with various degrees of competency to investigate and gather historic materials for almost every town and county. In most cases this material was then printed in booklet form and made available to the people living in the region.

In the early part of the twentieth century itinerant historians traveled from region to region collecting and writing histories of the areas for a price. Their special mode of operation was to write up the local history by giving sketches of the earlier pioneers, family by family. There was a major sales appeal to those whose families were thus immortalized. Copies of these early efforts are available in most regional libraries.

A third source of information may be found in various types of anniversary booklets. If the village celebrated a fiftieth or seventy-fifth anniversary, a history of the area usually was printed. The same is true of the churches that have been established from the early period of settlement.

In most communities a weekly newspaper was established quite early. Current events within the community were faithfully recorded. These papers usually make the best history of an area. However, it takes patience to read and glean pertinent materials.

In some of the younger communities the early settlers are still living. Usually they are pleased to give all the information that they can possibly remember. Every pastor ought to steep himself in the history of his community so that he may better comprehend why present-day conditions are as he finds them.

Understanding the Community — Its Activities

People living together in a community require various kinds of activities. The social relationships usually develop into many types of activities. In 1947 and 1948 representative community workers from various sections of the state participated in the Iowa Community Development Workshop. After carefully analyzing and classifying the activities in which communities engage, they pointed out the following eight as basic: (1) agriculture and conservation; (2) cultural arts and recreation; (3) education; (4) government (5) health; (6) home and family life; (7) industry and labor; (8) religious life.

In most communities these areas of activity just grow up like Topsy, with very little direction and little or no planning. Yet it is most significant that when these activities are out of proportion toward each other, or any one is entirely missing from the community life, stresses and strains develop which must be dealt with by all representative institutions functioning in the area. For example, many rural communities are almost totally lacking in recreational facilities. At best only two general types are available: The first, which takes care of that small group of athletes who make the "teams" in the local high school, leaves a large proportion of the population without any wholesome recreation. The second type is the kind that is found in the local tavern, which usually is questionable. This lack of adequate recreational facilities reflects itself directly on the job of the local church. If nothing is done by the church to meet this need, the youth work is bound to suffer at once and adult work will feel the impact in later years.

In many rural villages the economic opportunities are very inadequate. Farmers receive a good return for their labor, but young people growing up in the village have a very limited economic field to look to for life vocations. Thus, if the industry and labor activities in the local community are insufficient, the effect will immediately be felt in the church. The home and family will also suffer because young people will migrate as early as possible to areas where these activities are more plentiful.

The government of the rural community is usually quite unorganized and inadequate. Because of small population it is impractical to set up a government that will afford full-time positions and pay for its officers. Consequently, the part-time and volunteer officers cannot be so interested in nor trained for their positions as would otherwise be the case. This condition immediately reflects itself in the total life of the community. A good example of this came to the writer's attention. A small, unorganized village, located fourteen miles from an urban center having a population of 75,000 people, began to experience a wave of juvenile delinquency which showed itself in various ways. The young people accompanying the teams of the local township high school became very ill-mannered and unsportsmanlike when on trips away from home. Many drinking incidents became apparent. An unusual amount of property was maliciously destroyed. In quick succession four extremely unhappy sex cases came to light in the junior high school. The two churches in the town became greatly concerned. With the aid of the school superintendent investigations were started. The findings pointed to the same source. Several years earlier two roadhouses, because their proprietors had continued to ignore city ordinances, lost all their licenses to do business in the neighboring urban center. Because they were no longer able to function in their original location, they moved out to the village. One was located on the south edge, the other on the west edge, of town. Because there was not a strongly organized police force in the village, these roadhouses operated with almost no inhibitions. The youth in the village began to frequent them — delinquency was the result.

The pastor needs to understand these activities within the community. It is not easy to gather information that will make it possible for him to grasp thoroughly the implications of these activity areas. To attempt to gather the information alone is an all but impossible task. The pastor and his church are a part of the community; consequently, when action is taken, it ought to be with the co-operation of the other interested institutions and agencies that make up the total life of the community.

No single blueprint for the study of community needs and activities can be drawn up. Each case is different from any other. However, the first step in gathering information is similar in every case. A group of citizens representing different activities and interests gather to discuss the social structure of which they are a part. Such a committee might be made up of a pastor, school superintendent, farmer, banker, storekeeper, housewife, service station operator, and a doctor. It would help much to bring their thinking into the best possible focus if they had first read *Life in Montana,* by Brownell, Howard, and Meadows. The informal study group should then set up certain basic goals for which they are striving. One of the very best guides by which a community may be helpfully examined has been worked out by Extension Sociologist W. H. Stacy, of Iowa State College, Ames, Iowa. Under the name "Guides for Building Your Tomorrow's Community," Dr. Stacy has developed an eight-point testing program which is one of the most effective guides for study that the writer has ever seen. Every phase of this guide has carefully been tested in representative communities by responsible group leaders. In this guide Dr. Stacy has developed an outline which directs those interested toward a better understanding of the eight areas of activity discussed earlier. The characteristic that makes this guide superior is that the outline does not merely aid in finding facts, but also points out lines of action that, when followed, will strengthen the community. Results from studies such as these can point the way in which the program of the local church should be developed. Many times churches duplicate activities that are already being carried out satisfactorily by agencies within the community.

It would be much better for all if each church would develop some activity that has been entirely neglected in the area.

Understanding the Community — Its Structure

What is happening to the present population structure in our town and country areas will determine in a large measure what sort of church life can best be developed by the local pastor. To remain uninformed in this field is to ignore one of the most powerful influences at work in the church.

Recently a pastor and two members of his official church board came to visit me from a neighboring state. The congregation that he served had called him to be their pastor some eight years ago. At that time they received financial aid from the mission board of the denomination. The congregation agreed gradually to take over the major portion of their pastor's support. It was their purpose to be a self-supporting church in a period of ten years. During the first few years of the pastor's service, it was possible to reduce the outside aid according to the agreed schedule. However, during the past five years, the congregation could not meet this schedule. The Sunday school did not grow as had been anticipated. The church, numerically, was very little stronger than it had been when the pastor first came. There were no significant changes that could be noticed in the community. No other church had been started, the other existing churches had made no spectacular gain, and the area still seemed to be as prospective for church work as it had been eight years earlier. If a judgment had been passed on the minister, the congregation would have agreed that he was above average. He had no major antagonists among the members. Because it was not possible for the church to continue accepting the larger portion of the financial responsibility, the mission board had decided to cut off its support during the next year. The pastor and his committee presented this picture and hoped that somehow an explanation could be found for the problem which the church faced. A statistical study was agreed upon. Certain things came to light. The constituency of the church had a high average age. There were few child-bearing families. It was immediately evident that the church could not expect to grow from the inside. The public school record showed that almost two thirds of the young people left the community upon graduation from high school. The 1950 census also indicated that the population of the township in which the church was located had dropped 11 per cent. From these studies it became apparent that the church itself could not make sufficient growth to assume the additional financial burden suggested by the mission board. The real problem that both the mission board and the congregation faced was whether the church was meeting a real need in the area, and, if so, whether it justified an indefinite continuation of aid.

Very marked changes have taken place in the population structure of our rural communities. These changes are continuing and will continue for some years to come. The life of the rural church today depends upon an understanding of and an intelligent dealing with these changes. One of the best handbooks that the rural pastor could use today is the collection of statistical tables dealing with the population characteristics for his state. This document is available from the United States Government Printing Office, Washington, D. C. It is entitled *Population — General Characteristics* (State — Name).

The seventeenth census of the United States, taken in 1950, has indicated some facts that will have far-reaching significance in the total program of the rural church pastor. The rural farm population is shrinking. With large machinery, better roads, electricity, and hybrid seeds the farmer can and does take care of more land with less help than ever before. Because he has been able to take care of more land the number of farms has diminished, which also has caused farm population to become less. In the village the average age has increased. This means that people are growing older and different emphases must be made in the church's outreach program. The only rural area that is growing in numbers is the rural non-farm group. Around most cities large numbers of small homes are being developed — families who live on a few acres of ground have their work and business in the city. They are in the country, but not really of the country.

The rural churches that have their roots in the past have developed around the activities of the farmers and of the village tradesmen who serve the farmers. They have never had to deal with this new group; consequently many, if not most, of this group remain outside the church. In a recent religious survey (Iowa, 1946–1948, by Iowa Christian Rural Fellowship) the results showed that a twilight zone was developing around the urban centers. This twilight zone extended from the city limits to four or five miles out. In it were to be found this new group of our population. Since their interests, both economic and recreational were in the large population center, they did not participate in the religious life of the local rural church.

Another factor that is increasingly becoming evident in the study of the 1950 census is the migration of the people. To answer the question, " Where do the people go when they leave the farms and villages? " one needs to look at the population increases in the southwestern part of the United States. During the war years town and country boys for the first time became mobile. They were sent to Army and Navy camps all over the world. Many of them, who might normally never have experienced it, spent months in Arizona, California, Texas, and Florida. The climate pleased them. They decided that upon the war's end they would take their families and move into the newly found areas. When finally hostilities ended and these men returned to their homes, they put their decision into action. No longer would they spend weary days working on the fields of the Middle West; no longer would they endure the hardships of a northern winter. They actually moved by the hundreds of thousands. Thus the young life, so essential to the future of the old established rural churches, moved out.

Understanding the Community — Its Purpose

The American community when first developed usually had a good reason for its existence. Pioneers found a stream of water that could be dammed so that power for a mill might be obtained. Other services soon were centered in the same area and a village was born. Homes were built, schools and churches were organized, and a section of the population in the surrounding area looked to the new village as its community center.

Railroads began to build their roadbeds across the country. Switch tracks became necessary so that trains going in opposite directions might pass. Farmers found these locations strategic for shipping out their products; soon small villages developed and another community center was born.

The forested areas of the country developed sawmill villages which either gradually changed into farming villages or disappeared from the map. No matter what the purpose of the village originally was, the fact remains that when the community center loses its purpose or is unable to change its cause of existence with the developments and changes around it, the community becomes decadent.

At the present time there are a great number of such decadent villages. Once a railroad ran through the town, a sawmill was in operation, the flour mill was the center of industry. But all these have gone. Gradually the basic institutions cease to function. The school gradually becomes less effective and the church remains the last holdout to a dying cause. These changes do not happen overnight. They are of gradual development. Frequently the pastor of the church does not realize what is happening because he does not understand that the community has lost its purpose.

With transportation as elastic as it has become, with roads highly improved, and with county seat towns and urban centers offering the best of economic services, it sometimes becomes difficult to understand why the local community should continue to exist. Yet it has been pointed out frequently by sociologists and others that the personal life of people is deeply depleted when the community of which they once were a part has disintegrated. The human being needs to exist within a community and as part of a community if he is to have opportunity for the fullest expression of his social existence. In many rural communities, which are gradually disintegrating for lack of a purpose for existence, it is essential that a new purpose be found. That people will continue to live in the area is certain; that these people will continue to need the ministration of the church is likewise certain; it then becomes necessary for the remaining institutions and agencies to give new purpose to the entire cause of community. A successful example of how this was done in a decadent community was recorded by Richard Waverly Poston in *Small Town Renaissance,* covering the report on the Darby community in Montana.

If churches are to live and are to bring a vital service to their rural constituency, if programs are to be developed that will best meet the needs of all ages within the community, pastors will need to know their communities. To study the history, activities, structure, and purpose of the community will open the doors to a more useful and understanding ministry.

Chapter 3

STUDIES IN FAMILY

THE PATTERN of the rural family has always been a distinctive one. It is not possible in this limited description to give a complete picture of the development of the American rural family. Because of the widely scattered agricultural areas and the distinctive type of agricultural pursuits there are many specifics that could be explained. However, it is best to give general impressions that might fit most agrarian types. The rural family has always been a strong one. This has resulted from the need for the family to be self-sufficient in most ways. With the isolation of the early farmsteads, absence of good roads, and slow and uncertain transportation, the family had to find within itself most of the major satisfactions of life. Consequently, the rural family was much stronger in its ties than the urban.

The rural family was usually large. In the early days when land was cheap and homesteads were the usual source of property, it was almost impossible to obtain labor for agricultural chores or domestic affairs. Yet the agrarian way of life, before the advent of the machine, demanded a great deal of help. The best source for this help lay in the family potential itself. Families of five, six, and seven were the rule; it was not unusual to find a family of twelve children. Boys were always hailed with delight; girls, as a necessary source of help for the mother. There was an early saying which has been handed down to us that on the land a son was worth one thousand dollars and a daughter five hundred dollars. In the urban areas, even at so early a period, children were considered an economic liability rather than an asset. Today, in examining our church buildings that have been handed down to us from the earlier generation, we find one fact standing out, namely, the large seating capacity of the main worship room. Today in many of these churches only half the pews are occupied on the Sabbath, or even less. There are grandfathers and grandmothers who remember when the churches were filled to capacity. This does not necessarily mean that the attendance was much more regular in those days. It would rather reflect the size of the family and the limited sources of recreation.

The church was the chief center of attraction to the rural family. Moving pictures had not been developed, roller skating rinks were unheard of, dance pavilions were few and very far between, school buildings were small and scattered; consequently, the family turned to the church, not only for religious instruction, but also for social expression. The author in speaking to some of the earlier pioneer settlers of the Dakotas, Nebraska, and western Iowa, has again and again been amazed by the constant emphasis that these oldsters have put on the memory of two major experiences of their lives. The first of these centered always in the church; the second, in the weekly trip into the neighboring village for the purchase of provisions and the exchange of news and gossip.

The school also played an important role in the life of the early rural family. So long as a family had children in the local one-room grade school, the interest of that family centered itself, so far as neighborhood affairs were concerned, in that school district. Several times during each school year it became the practice of the families to gather for a program of recitations and songs delivered by the children. Kerosene lamps lighted the festive occasion and usually a lunch was served after the program. This gave the neighborhood families just another opportunity for social contact.

Factors that have been mentioned before, namely, isolation of the rural family, poor modes of transportation, and inadequate roads, in themselves were factors to cause the rural family to resist change. There were other factors of equal importance. Usually when a group of people migrated from their homeland in Europe and settled on farms and in little villages, they tried to maintain the homeland language and customs. The first generation of settlers succeeded well. The second generation also continued this practice. The barrier of language and of nationality did much in the earlier days to develop in the rural family a frame of mind that resisted change.

This resistance to change was especially noticeable in the area of economic welfare. The rural family was more willing to change its technique of agriculture than its mode of communication. This does not mean that the rural family did not resist mechanization. In the early history of mechanization, however, such resistance was much more apparent in the noneconomic areas. This unwillingness to change became the butt of many cartoons and jokes among the more urbane. The farmer became a " hayseed," the villager a " stick-in-the-mud," and in general, they and their families were " rubes." The church that served the rural family also shared this reputation. As a consequence, most seminary graduates, after having spent years of their lives in education, usually in schools in urban areas, looked at the rural church as an institution from which to stay away. At best, they considered it as a legitimate, experimental ground: a place in which to get experience so that it would be possible to get a better church in an urban area. The saying got around, " If you have to make mistakes as a young preacher, you had better make them in the country church where it doesn't make any difference."

Because of the stability of the rural people and the rather unchanging quality of the rural community, the family on the land and in the village went through the four stages of development usually without migration.

The first phase: The rural family passed through a childless period. This was the time in which the land was first rented, or the son, recently married, took over the home farm, or by some good fortune the young couple were able to purchase land, or they hired themselves out as a tenant family. Economically, this was one of the most difficult of the four phases. Money was hard to come by and the strain of getting started was most severe.

The second phase followed swiftly upon the heels of the first. It was the period in which the family took root. Children were born, and for a number of years were unable to make a significant contribution through their labors. This was the phase when the mother and the father found their young strength taxed to the limit. During the day it meant constant physical labor expended on the land, among the animals, and in the home. At night it frequently meant waking hours with little children. During this period the economic foundations of the family were being drawn and laid.

The third phase started when the children began to make their contribution to the economic welfare of the family. The boys made their contribution on the land and the girls within the home. At this period the cultural roots of the entire family, and the cultural influence of the community, were deeply implanted in these children. The rural church became the most important institution in the life of the family. If ever the family was able to win economic security, it was during this time. With a total contribution of all the children, larger areas of land could be worked. Frequently one family possessed and developed an entire section of land. It was in this period that the ultimate economic strength was developed.

The fourth phase of the rural family was one of decline. Children who had been so much of strength to the parents were married and developed families of their own. Some of them remained in the immediate neighborhood, but as land became scarcer they were forced to move to more distant areas. More and more the children found it necessary to turn to another type of employment in adjacent towns and even distant cities. It was during this period that the again childless family retired, usually to the village in which the church was situated.

The rural family developed a oneness and solidarity as a result of its unified interest and its limited horizons. In many areas it was not unusual for the family to develop into a sort of tribal unit. Older children who had become established on land helped the younger children to get a start. Decisions were made in family consultation. This down-to-earth solidarity resulted in a very stable, although somewhat unyielding, church congregation.

With the introduction and the exceeding rapid development of agricultural machinery, the entire picture of the rural family and its village counterpart underwent a metamorphosis. Tractors and power machinery replaced the need for sons on the land. Electricity and other modern conveniences made daughters less necessary. All-weather roads wound their ways not only into the geographical countryside but also into the cultural structure of the community. The rural family felt the powerful impact of the machine age most intimately within the family circle. Machines made fathers' work much more productive and voluminous. Consequently, sons who had been worth "a thousand dollars" now tended toward being liabilities. They were sent to school to be educated for tasks other than the land. In almost direct proportion to the utilization of machines, the family fertility decreased. The trend was toward smaller families.

The cultural lag between the rural and urban families was completely annihilated. The same type of dresses as were for sale in New York City could be purchased through the Sears, Roebuck catalogue. The farmer's wife no longer appeared dated by her clothes. She was as stylishly dressed as was her city cousin. Radios brought into the country and the small village home the same programs that were produced and received in the urban area. With the better modes of transportation, the rural family was no longer isolated in its section of the country. Members of the family began to travel first to the county seat, later to the nearest large city, then to the national parks, and finally to any section of the country that they desired to see. All sorts of recreational facilities, professional entertainment, and social expression became possible to them. Because in so short a time, actually the span of one generation, the cultural changes were so enormous, the rural family suffered the shock of disintegration. For many years the urban family had already gone through processes of disintegration which resulted from divers interests, separate jobs, individual friendships, etc. The rural family only recently began to experience the impact of this change. The rural church, which had been just as resistant to change as the rural family, lagged behind in adapting itself to the new situation forced upon it by the machine age. Today there is a mass of unanswered questions that must be dealt with if the rural family is to retain its rightful heritage. Likewise, the rural church must be prepared, not merely to face the changes brought upon it by its constituency, but actually to forge ahead in the spirit of the early pioneers to solve the problems confronting it.

For many years there has been a general misapprehension about the health of the rural family. Because of the nature of his work, the rural worker was usually considered to be healthier than his urban cousin. However, after many studies made by various Government agencies, it became evident that this apparent situation of good health did not exist. Fred A. Mott wrote in the *Journal of the American Medical Association,* 1946: "As of 1940 we find that the infectious and more or less preventable diseases take larger rural tolls. If we consider the most rural state and the most urban state in each of the nine census regions, we find that, as a group, the most rural states had higher case rates in 1942 for chicken pox, whooping cough, mumps, scarlet fever, diphtheria, septic sore throat, malaria, bacillary dysentery, typhoid and paratyphoid, tularemia, and smallpox. Trends show that tuberculosis and syphilis may soon become primarily rural." There are some easily defined reasons for this prevalence of preventable diseases in the rural areas.

The first of these is the fact that for many years the rural person was able to acquire less cash for his farming and business operation than the urban worker. Medical services have always been high. Before expending an essential portion of its cash for medical services, the rural family delayed as long as possible. Consequently, preventable diseases were allowed to run their course and resulted in many more losses of the day's work than in the city.

Another contributing reason comes from the fact that there are considerably fewer doctors per number of population in the country than in the city. There is 1 doctor for every 580 people in the city. In the country there is 1 doctor for every 1,336 people. In Minnesota, for example, in 1936 there was 1 doctor for every 1,814 rural people. On the other hand, in Minnesota's urban areas there was 1 doctor for every 434 people. The case load that the rural physician has always had to carry has been much greater than that in the cities. It might also be pointed out that the physicians who remain in rural areas are as a whole older than those in urban areas. The younger physician who starts in the rural area is very mobile and soon moves out.

Another contributing difficulty has been the lack of hospital space for rural people. Hospitals have been located without much consideration of rural population. Studies that have recently been made indicate that for every hospital bed available in the rural areas there are three available in the urban area. Coupled to this is the fact that farm homes and villages are widely separated and quite isolated. Thus it can readily be seen that the health situation in rural areas leaves much to be desired. Probably as a consequence of isolation and other factors mentioned in this chapter, rural families more frequently use home remedies that are based upon superstition rather than upon curing qualities. It is not at all unusual for these superstitions to become a part of the cultural acceptance of an area. Among the people of one large rural settlement in Iowa it was customary for parents to sew a band of black velvet around the throat of a teething infant. This velvet supposedly had the curative quality of making the process of teething easier and causing the pain to diminish. It was not good practice to take this band off at any time during teething.

Again it becomes apparent that in this area of rural life the church must concern itself. The cure of the body runs hand in hand in importance with the cure of the soul.

Another factor that has added to disconcerting problems of rural life has been the Second World War, with its abortive child, the Korean conflict. Because the rural family continues to maintain a numeric advantage over the urban family, it has also made, proportionately, a larger contribution by the sacrifice of its man power to the defense of its country. Both boys and girls, young men and young women, have been released from the village and the farm to man the armed services of our land. From limited horizons, through their new experiences they were compelled to take in a world view. The local farm and village community became an experience rather than an end in life. As they were moved from one section of the world to another, they discovered geographical areas that gave them more physical satisfaction than anything had before. Many determined to give up citizenship in the old rural community upon their return to civilian life for a new mode of living in an area of the country which they considered more favorable. Thus, the disintegration of the rural family was speeded. In the recent U.S. census (1950), it has become evident that the rural community that is not centered by a city of 2,500 population or more is declining numerically. At the same time it is also evident that the same area, agriculturally speaking, produces more than before the period of population decline, which is again evidence that fewer hands with larger and more efficient machines are able to produce more products than before. However, this factor has also caused the rural church to decline and is causing the church and its organizations to face a problem which on the surface seems insuperable.

With the development of complex machinery, the need for a thorough education has become evident. Professional schools and liberal arts colleges have changed their courses to meet the new experiences of people. Rural families, which for many years were underprivileged economically, have experienced a new freedom as a result of greater incomes. Education, which formerly, to a great extent, was considered a luxury by the rural family, something to be desired but attained only by the privileged few, has suddenly become a necessity. Consequently, many children who would otherwise have been absorbed on the farms or in the villages now receive professional education and find a new mode of living in some urban area. This is just another of the many forces that are striking at the older concepts of the rural family.

During the depression years 1929–1936, the farm and village family suffered almost irreparable damage. Farm families lost their land through foreclosure and were dispossessed by the thousands. The village family that was entirely dependent upon its farm trade suffered to the same extent. The history is an old and familiar one. Gradually the Government was forced to take action. Mortgage moratoriums were declared. Farm loans through the Farm Security Administration were made possible. Price supports became acceptable procedures. Conservation practices were underwritten by the Federal Administration. A formula for parity prices was developed. A new type of Government-induced farm security became the accepted practice for farm and village families.

Because of the new financial subsidization by the Federal Government, a greater burden of taxation became essential and mandatory. For the price of economic security the rural family had to pay by the surrender of a proportionate part of its independence. That which the family once considered its private business and its absolute right during the time that it was isolated now had to be open to the public eye; at least the records had to be carefully kept and submitted to the scrutiny of a patronizing Government. This most recent development in the experience of the rural family has also had its influence upon the surrender of old economic concepts and cultural patterns.

The rural family, with its old institutions and organizations now emerging under an entirely new concept of public and private relationships, is faced with many questions that can best be answered on the grounds of a theological ethic. This places the responsibility for many of the major answers in the hands of the rural church and its leadership.

Chapter 4

STUDIES IN THE LOCAL CHURCH

IT IS DIFFICULT to describe the early development of the rural church which took place hand in hand with the pioneer settlement of population. First in the New England states, then along the Atlantic seaboard, and gradually in the Midwest and the plains states, this settlement took place. In early pioneer movements three institutions were always present: homes were built first to house the families and to give a locale of operation; churches and schools came next. Pioneer families were anxious to have education as part of the total picture of life. Consequently they located schools convenient to their homesteads. Churches were also of primary concern. Their construction always took place early in each settlement. Many of the rural churches were placed upon the land conveniently located to the families that were interested. As villages developed, churches were also located in the villages. Because of poor transportation it was best for the early settlers that churches should be convenient to their farmsteads. A five-mile drive by team and wagon was almost too much. In one county of Iowa it was the ambition of an early bishop of the Roman Catholic Church to have a congregation established within driving range of each family. He took his team of horses and drove from place to place; the location of churches was determined by the length of time it took him to drive. Today in that county, these churches are still standing, located on prominent hills approximately five miles apart.

The natural desire of the pioneers to have churches within easy driving range resulted in one of two situations. The first: In many instances there were too many rural churches, far beyond the need of the population. This was especially true after roads were improved and automobiles took the place of horses. The second: Churches became neighborhood churches instead of serving a large area. Families and closely knit racial groups rallied around each local church. Their ties were so close that when the time came for change and it was manifest that changes should be made, neighborhood groups resisted it.

Recently the author stood on a high ridge overlooking the countryside for miles around. A cement highway wound along the ridge and gradually dipped down into the valley. Gravel roads left the highway at right angles or forked off across hills and valleys connecting all the farmsteads within view. Gradually as the sun set and night rose out of the valley to cover the hills, lights twinkled on in every direction. The surrounding territory appeared like some great town suddenly drawn together. Less than ten years ago this same area had no paved roads; side roads were impassable much of the year; farmsteads were isolated from each other and from the market place; and at night there were no lights of friendliness that could be seen across the entire countryside.

The impact of modernization and mechanization has been almost unbelievable within the structure of the family itself. As we have noted before, in less than a generation the habits of centuries were changed. The rural churches, which had been geared to the slower tempo of life, did not change at the same rate. It almost seemed as though the more rapid the cultural change of the people, the more resistant to that change the church and its leadership became.

Today it is quite apparent that certain basic problems that have arisen within the structure of the church must be met. The remainder of this chapter will concern itself with these.

1. *The Theological Problem*

The pioneers that came from Europe, especially those who settled in rural villages and on the land itself, left their homeland for one of several reasons. Most prominent among these reasons were: (1) Their inability to climb the ladder of economic success in Europe. The class distinction frequently based upon occupation made it impossible for young people to move from one class to another. To many of these, America seemed the land of opportunity. As soon as it was possible to acquire sufficient money to pay passage to the

United States, groups would get together and leave their homeland. (2) There were also persecuted groups in Europe that were anxious to leave for America to establish new homes and achieve new opportunities for both themselves and their children. These too would gather in groups and leave their homeland. (3) Compulsory military training had become one of the fixed traditions of many central and northern European countries. Many people objected to compulsory military service. If they had growing sons in their families, they would sell everything they had to get passage to the United States where compulsory military service was unheard of.

The experience of these groups in the United States was not easy. They soon discovered that the streets were not paved with pure gold and that silver dollars did not grow on trees. In fact, many of them found that making a living in the United States was even more difficult than it was in Europe. The country was wild; the health services and protective forces were few and far between. The weather, especially in continental United States, was exceedingly severe. In many sections of New England, Wisconsin, Minnesota, and the Dakotas the winters were far colder than any these settlers had experienced before. It was natural that as a result of these difficulties the interpretation of theology was very rigid, exacting, and puritanical. Since they had not found in the United States the kingdom of plenty, they felt that God had reserved it for the next world. This resulted in an otherworldliness with which their preaching, conversation, and hymns were filled. This feeling was expressed by Fanny J. Crosby in her hymn called " Blessed Homeland."

" Gliding o'er life's fitful waters
Heavy surges sometimes roll,
And we sigh for yonder haven,
For the homeland of the soul.

Refrain:
" Blessed homeland, ever fair!
Sin can never enter there,
But the soul to life awaking
Everlasting bloom shall wear.

"Oft we catch a faint reflection
Of its bright and vernal hills,
And though distant, how we hail it!
How each heart with rapture thrills!

"To our Father, and our Saviour,
To the Spirit, three in one,
We shall sing glad songs of triumph
When our harvest work is done.

"'Tis the weary pilgrim's homeland
Where each throbbing care shall cease,
And our longings and our yearnings
Like a wave, be hushed to peace."

In order that the "pilgrim" of this earth might achieve the happy homeland, he needed to obey the rules and regulations that were laid down by the church leaders as a result of their rigid theological interpretations. The religious pietism which gradually developed into an unchanging theological conservatism was a natural result of this attitude. Gradually as the pioneer fathers gave way to newer generations and the wilderness continent of the United States was conquered, many of the sufferings and privations experienced by the early settlers no longer existed. Comforts, pleasures, recreation, and materialistic gain, which had been altogether impossible before, were now common. The rural church has resisted the need to reinterpret its theological dogmas in the light of its new surroundings. This resistance has tended to push the rural church away from the axis of life out into the peripheral circle. This inflexibility within the church has resulted in a second major problem.

2. *The Community Problem*

Early in its existence the American church found itself in an exceedingly strategic position. It was the most thoroughly accepted institution in the community. Its voice was usually listened to when it spoke concerning public affairs and community agencies. However, that voice was dimmed as the church held onto its traditional position and refused to recognize both the impact and the validity of mechanistic change. When it continued to sing about the city of "pure gold" for which the heart longed and to preach about this "vast vale of tears" below, and taught that the earth was a den of iniquity and vice, young people began to leave its fold. They found a new emotional enjoyment at the roller skating rink and a deep satisfaction in the streets that were paved with cement rather than gold. Thus, gradually, the church, with its needed influence, was weeded out of the center of community activity and pushed aside. Of course, people still thought of it as a good moral institution, a place to which they could send children so that they might acquire good ethical standards. But the church was no longer the heart of the community.

Peculiarly enough, the second primary institution that had developed hand in hand with the church now received the attention and good will of the community. That was the public school system. Each neighborhood had its rural school; each community developed its independent school district and then, in more recent years, its consolidated school or township school. The major social activities of rural families were transferred from the church to the school. Debate teams, drama productions, and athletic contests demanded the loyalty of the family to a greater extent than the church could now achieve. During this period a marked decline took place in the rural church. It became increasingly difficult to get adequately trained leaders. It was a much more difficult problem to catch the imagination of lay leadership. No longer did community agencies turn to the church for advice and guidance.

Another step has come about in recent years which will eventually take the development of local leadership away from the schools. Consolidation of public institutions into larger centers and even larger institutions is happening all over as a result of new state-aid laws recently enacted. The excuses given for this consolidation are based upon economies of operation, efficiency of administration, and effectiveness of instruction. The United States has been going through a period in which its people have been impressed by the grandeur of bigness. This philosophy is catching up with our educational institutions. It is said that a small high school is not able to give good instruction. It is not economically sound. Since roads and transportation are no longer a barrier, it is relatively simple to transport all children to these larger institutions. Consequently, the schools which for so long a period of time had been centers of the communities' activities are now losing that privilege even as the rural churches lost it earlier. The real problem that now ensues is this: What shall now be the heart of the community? The church is still there; the school is on the move. One other agency has taken a deep hold on the community, and conceivably might make a bid for this position. It is the fast developing neighborhood and community tavern. With right leadership the rural church might again regain its former position.

3. *The Leadership Problem*

The early rural church was blessed with a very able ministry. Because living had not been complicated by excess mechanization, the agrarian way of life was predominant. Most of our country was rural. Its institutions, its families, its outlook were all geared to the slow pace of the farmer and his relationship to the natural resources. Education was classical rather than utilitarian. It prepared leadership to understand man in his relationship to God and these natural resources. As a consequence, the pastoral leadership of the early rural church was very able. Because of the pastor's learning and understanding, he held a place of high esteem within the community. His word was considered of great value in the development of community enterprises. Frequently, he was the adviser and arbitrator in temporal affairs as well as spiritual. Schools of higher learning were especially geared to the preparation of pastors. Much of the printed material in the form of books and periodicals that got into the hands of our pioneers was produced by the pastors of those early churches.

With the rapid shift of emphasis away from the rural area to the ways of commerce and industry which were centered in the larger cities, the rural church lost its leadership. It was natural that during a time of rapid development people should focus their attention upon the mechanical genius of man. Agriculture seemed relatively unimportant. The wheel and the lever loomed much more powerful in the eyes of men than the resources out of which the wheel and the lever were made. Education made a complete about-face. Leaders had to be prepared for industry. The city was now the important focal point. Population began to move from the country with its villages to the cities. Institutional churches were springing up within these cities. Large membership rolls were achieved. Salaries were high. Rural pastors were anxious to move up a mythical ladder of success into a city church. Young men preparing themselves for the ministry would not consider the rural church. During this period thousands of rural churches throughout the land became pastorless. Without leadership, these churches could not exist. It has been said by various authorities that ten thousand rural churches closed their doors. Denomination after denomination gradually became aware of the problem. At first it was a rather careless awareness. Some of the denominational leaders have said that most of the rural churches ought to be closed, that unless a church has five hundred members it cannot be an effective church. Such loose thinking continued the assault upon the rural church. By 1935 it became apparent that a complete about-face had to be made, otherwise even the urban church would lose its source of membership.

One of the first problems connected with this awareness that had to be solved was that of leadership. Would it be possible as in years gone by to prepare a general leadership for the church without any specific training in rural concepts? Would it be necessary to develop an indigenous leadership for the rural church? More and more the rural people expressed themselves as dissatisfied with uninformed general pastoral leadership. An elder in a rural Presbyterian church gave vent to his feelings in the following manner: "What kind of leadership is being developed for our Church? We had our new preacher out for dinner the other Sunday. He called my new hay chopper a manure spreader." Many of the seminaries, sensing this need and challenge, are developing courses that aid in the preparation of rural pastors. A few of the schools sense that a number of courses tacked onto the usual curriculum are not sufficient to prepare pastors for rural areas. These schools now feel that a completely integrated program of education in all the traditional fields of theological education is necessary. In case students have had no background in rural life itself, the seminaries are giving them opportunity to take survey courses in agricultural colleges in preparation for a better-informed ministry to rural people. Because of the more difficult problem of co-operation, with which we shall deal in a later chapter, a large number of young men are preparing themselves for life careers in rural church work even as missionaries prepare themselves for mission fields. It is in this area of leadership that a new and great hope is developing for rural people.

4. *The Youth Problem*

It is not difficult to discover that an organization that seeks to perpetuate itself must at some time or other deal realistically with a youth program. The young people have always been one of the church's chief sources of strength. After the development of the Sunday school a great proportion of the membership of the church was recruited directly out of this school. The church that has lost the support, interest, and attendance of young people has been cut loose from its source of membership supply. In this regard the history and development of the rural church in America has been very spotty. In the earlier years the church needed to make no direct effort at holding its youth, nor did it need to develop a program of special emphasis for this age group. As has been noted before, the chief social outlet for our pioneers was to be found directly in the activities of the church, even though these activities were predominantly and primarily spiritual in nature. The old camp ground evangelistic meetings were a great rallying place for young and old alike. Many can look back with nostalgia on those early days, for at an evangelistic meeting either at the church or at the camp ground they first became acquainted with the persons who later became their life partners. The old singing school, which had not as yet been named "choir practice evening," was also a favorite source of social interrelationship for youth. Actually, there was little or nothing to compete with the church for the time and interest of young people.

For hundreds of years the church had a free hand in this matter. The sudden and cataclysmic change of the first half of the twentieth century altered this entire picture almost overnight. Every possible center of population developed commercialized entertainment, with young people particularly the target. The moving picture industry eventually developed in almost every county seat town and even in many smaller villages. Especially, young people drove in to these centers from miles around to participate vicariously in the new and romantic world of the cinema. With the introduction of new standards of conduct and morality through moving pictures, the dance hall was also able to develop in the otherwise puritanical area. The church, sensing the gradual loss of its youth to commercialized amusements, became incensed. With more emotional feeling than good sense, it attacked through both the preaching of the Word and its publication every form of commercial amusement. Young people were particularly condemned for their interest and participation. This condemnation on the part of the church rather than frightening them into better co-operation with the church estranged them instead. An entire generation of young people became lost to the church. It has been the experience of most organizations that to condemn without replacement is to lose completely. Recent studies that have been made indicate to what an extent this alienation of young people has taken place.

Shortly before the Second World War several thousand young people chosen at random from more than forty counties in the State of Iowa were contacted by the author. Although a high percentage of the group had attended Sunday school, they had dropped out of the church before their sixteenth year. They had not looked to the church as the source of their social contacts. Four-H clubs, Rural Young People's Assembly, the movies, and roller skating rinks were the most common places mentioned in which to find social gratification.

A recent study completed in 1952 by the Rural Church Department of the Theological Seminary of the University of Dubuque covered a large segment of Grant County, Wisconsin, including 427 rural families and 974 urban families. From this study it also became very evident that the urban churches were doing, and had done, a much better job of youth conservation than the rural churches. It is evident from Tables 1 and 2, page 49, that the 4-H clubs are doing a better job in contacting young people than the church is accomplishing.

The inevitable conclusion must be that in regard to young people the rural church has failed to measure up to the high standard it once held. It also appears as though it will be doubly difficult for the church to re-establish a right relationship with young people, having lost it for a generation. This loss of its vital interest in young people is now posing a problem to religious leadership that can be solved only by exceedingly careful planning and by establishing a

Table 1

RURAL YOUNG PEOPLE

Age	Total Number	Number in Church Youth Organizations	Number in Secular Youth Organizations
10-14	187	15	61
15-19	134	32	60
Total 10-19	321	47	121

Table 2

URBAN YOUNG PEOPLE

Age	Total Number	Number in Church Youth Organizations	Number in Secular Youth Organizations
10-14	203	59	80
15-19	193	58	42
Total 10-19	396	117	122

new and more vital concept of the church and its task in the hearts of a new generation.

5. *The Stewardship Problem*

The pioneer community depended more upon barter and trade than it did on cash. Men would barter their services for some of the necessities of life. Very frequently each person shared hours of labor with his neighbor in exchange for labor when needed. Little cash changed hands because there was little to be had. The early rural pastor fitted into this pattern even better than most. Usually a minimum stipend in cash was promised the minister. The remainder of his income was " in kind." The author's father served as one of the early pastors in the southwest corner of Minnesota and the northwest corner of Iowa. Even in the late nineties, his experience followed this pattern. He received $298 for a year's salary. Potatoes and flour were assured gifts. Hay and grain for a horse were also given. Meat was supplied by families whenever they butchered. If wood was available, a supply was brought to him. It was a precarious living at best.

The custom of ten per cent discount to pastors was established at this time. As parishioners gave a portion of their produce to the pastors, the merchant gave a special discount on cash purchases. Although there were many needs in the pastor's home that were never met, most of his parishioners were going through similar experiences so it was not difficult to face these privations together.

Another point should be made in this place. Most of these rural churches were established with the help of home mission monies which were raised by more established churches, usually in the eastern section of the country. Offerings were taken by established congregations, and loans were made by mission boards, to make possible the erection of these new churches. In many cases the pastor was also subsidized by such funds. The church thus established and developed frequently tried to hold onto this outside aid as long as possible. In this way a smaller drain would be made on the financial capacities of the church families.

When change was made from hand and horse power to steam, gasoline, and electricity, the need for more cash with which to do business was immediately felt. The entire economic structure of the country underwent a remarkable change. People no longer went about trading services and bartering goods. A farmer sold his grain, cattle, and dairy products for cash. He purchased his supplies, new machinery, and services of labor for cash. Hence it became necessary to pay the pastor on a different basis. Instead of a horse, he now kept a car. He was expected to be as well dressed as other professional men. He needed to keep his rightful place in the community. Salaries were raised, but for many years the rural pastor's salary was far below the level that it should have been. He was kept poor and thereby very humble. The result of this treatment was that many pastors who were able to move from a rural to an urban church did so as rapidly as possible. In the urban church, the professional man and laborer recognized the validity of better financial support for the pastor. The differential of salary between rural and urban pastors was exceedingly great.

At the same time that this was occurring, the old frame church buildings that had been erected by the pioneers proved inadequate. The same was true of the parsonages. This resulted in a building program. It cost many times more to erect new buildings than it had cost to build the first structures in which the rural families had worshiped. Many congregations went into debt as a consequence. The over-all picture of the rural church during this period was rather dismal. The financial structure was not only inadequate but also insecure. Furthermore, at this time an appeal was made by the various denominations for monies by which to strengthen their foreign missionary enterprises and to develop their colleges to meet the new needs of a new age. Most of the rural churches whose families had not learned a consecrated stewardship fell far short of their rightful share.

Of course, there were exceptions. Many strong congregations whose main constituents were to be found among descendants of the Germans and the Scandinavians rose to the challenge of the denomination. But, in the over-all picture of the rural church in the United States, the obligations of the families to this challenge of stewardship were most inadequately met. The dependence of the rural family upon the land and the weather for financial success, and the harrowing experiences of the depression of the thirties, developed a deep caution, especially in this matter of giving. In these recent years the economic status of the rural family has developed with exceeding rapidity. Farm poverty gave way to farm prosperity. Land mortgages disappeared. A new-found wealth became apparent on almost every hand. From this it would appear that the stewardship obligations of the rural church would now certainly be more adequately fulfilled. This has not been the case. The rise in stewardship responsibility on the part of rural people did not compare to the rapid rise in their personal incomes. This continues to be both a problem and a puzzle to the student who would like to understand it. Although in certain sections where agriculture has become an almost prosperous industry rural pastors are being paid an adequate salary, the overall picture is still dismal. The rural church must meet and solve the problem of inadequate stewardship on the part of its people.

6. *The Outreach Problem*

The early structure of the rural church was largely dependent upon immigrant groups. For example, East Frisians who settled in one area developed their church. The Scots who settled adjacent to them developed another church. The Germans who settled not far distant developed a third church. Each of these churches ministered to the group that originally developed it. For almost two generations there was little crossing of these racial or nationalistic lines. The growth of the church did not depend upon an outreach program, but rather upon internal growth. Families were large, and land in the area was available. Children, as they grew to adulthood, married within the national group and settled in the immediate area. Thus, these churches experienced a consistent growth in those first years. During the period of the second and third generations a change came about. The East Frisians, the Scots, the Germans, and others began to intermarry. Language lines were obliterated. Churches that had served and depended for their growth upon racial groups no longer had this source for a growing constituency. During this period many churches began a decline that resulted in the closing of hundreds and thousands of them in the Midwest. Table 3, page 53, gives a picture of what happened in one denomination alone, the Presbyterian Church, U.S.A.

The intermarriage between nationalities and the inclination on the part of the churches to hold onto their foreign-language services resulted in many families' having either only a nominal church relationship or none whatsoever. The birth rate also declined so that large families were no longer popular. Thus an internal growth in the church was no longer possible. Gradually, it came to the attention of churches that a new type of outreach program had to be developed.

Table 3

TOTAL NUMBER OF CHURCHES LOST DURING 50-YEAR PERIOD

1900-1950 ACCORDING TO STATES

States	Number Lost	Percentage of Total
Iowa	119	25
Nebraska	77	31
Kansas	144	39
Missouri	236	45
North Dakota	99	47
South Dakota	51	29
Minnesota	104	30
Arkansas	65	53
Oklahoma	109	45
Total	1,004	

The rural people have for many years borne the reputation of harboring little prejudice. This reputation, however, was built upon theory rather than fact. It was exceedingly difficult, and in many areas today remains exceedingly difficult, for a rural church that developed on a nationality basis to reach out among people of other races or other nationalities for a new constituency. An example of this occurred in the late thirties. A new church that was independent of denominations had been organized and developed in a mixed Scandinavian community. This church had drawn into its membership the non-Scandinavian people and such people as through mixed marriages were without a church home. After some years of independence this church made overtures to a denomination of Norwegian background for entry. In the discussions that followed, several of the denominational leaders repeatedly brought up this problem, "Can this church which is not Norwegian really become a part of us?"

The need for an adequate outreach program has grown as a result of a large proportion of rural population without church affiliation and the present-day amazing mobility of families. (It has been estimated that in the stable Middle West twenty-five per cent of the rural population moves every four years.) This problem presents the greatest present challenge to the rural church.

7. *The Overchurching Problem*

In almost every book that has been written about the town and country church, and in many of the better-known books on rural sociology, one of the statements frequently made is that the town and country area is woefully overchurched. All sorts of facts are given as proof for this assertion. There can be little doubt about the truth of these. So long as churches cater to a certain nationalistic group within the community and the population within the rural area steadily declines, the problem of overchurching becomes even more acute. On the other hand, in many studies that have been completed in Iowa, Minnesota, Wisconsin, and Illinois, the picture presents itself in a somewhat different fashion. In most rural counties studied, in which no major urban center is located, the churches are mislocated rather than too numerous.

By adding together the total seating capacity of all the churches in a county, one finds that if one half the population of that county twelve years of age and above should want to attend church on any given Sunday, the seating capacity would not handle the crowds. In such a study it will become evident that in some communities there will be more than adequate seating capacity in the churches while in other areas this capacity will be totally inadequate. Consequently the rural church faces a rather difficult problem, namely, that in certain rural areas there are too many churches, while in other areas church facilities are inadequate.

Part Two

BUILDING THE PROGRAM

Chapter 5

ANALYZING AND INTERPRETING THE STEPS

THE ACTUAL BUILDING of any program must be predicated upon the architect's knowledge of the background and conditions out of which the need for planning grows. In both city and rural churches a sort of traditional program has been handed down from generation to generation. If a careful analytic study could be made of the curriculums of theological seminaries that have been in existence two hundred or more years, it would be discovered that basically these curriculums have had little change. Some subjects naturally have been added. In the last few years an attempt has been made by seminaries to reinterpret and redefine the aims and purposes of theological education.

This resistance to change on the part of theological seminaries has resulted in a ministry whose pattern has also resisted change. Consequently, many pastors have gone, and continue to go, to new parishes with the idea that the program administered in years past would fit any situation. Without studying the church in its environment, they attempt to carry on a program irrelevant to the needs of the community, its families and people. The turbulent change that has taken place in rural America as a result of mechanization has also brought about a revolution in the cultural life and the moral needs of its people, as has been pictured elsewhere in this book. These changes play a very important part in the programing of the church.

One of the richest sources of information to help an incoming pastor—or, for that matter, the pastor who has been on the field for some years—is the records kept on the local church level. Many pastors have complained that these records have been kept so poorly that it is almost impossible to follow them chronologically. However, most of them are to be found in permanent form in the annual reports of the various denominations. These yearbooks with amazing regularity give information in four vital areas of the church's life. The first of these is the area of church membership. By a study of the church records, a twenty-five-year graph can easily be worked out, showing the rise and fall numerically of the membership of a given church. The second area, which is also to be found in the yearbook, is that of Sunday school membership. Some denominational yearbooks also record the Sunday school membership over against average attendance. The rise and fall of this membership can be plotted upon a chart. Two other vital areas that can readily be found are those of local congregational expense and benevolent giving to world-wide objects of benevolence, such as missions, colleges, seminaries, etc.

Using the Cross Roads Federated Church, the author acquired the self-explanatory data shown in Table 4 taken from the records of the past twenty-five years.

The condition of the Cross Roads Federated Church can be further visualized through the use of graphs comparing local church expenses with benevolences, and church membership with church school enrollment.

In interpreting these figures and graphs, there are certain things that must be carefully weighed. The first of these are the population trends during the past twenty or thirty years. In rural areas near county seat and/or urban centers, the population has shown a marked increase. The percentage of population increase during the period covered by the study must be balanced against the increase in church membership and Sunday school enrollment. On the other hand, in many rural areas that are not near urban centers the population has decreased during the past thirty years. This decrease of population must also be considered in the light of increase or decrease in church membership and Sunday school enrollment.

Secondly, it is easy to be misled by apparent increases in the financial structure of a church. Almost all churches have shown a decided increase in giving toward congregational expenses and benevolent

Table 4

FOUR AREA 25-YEAR CHURCH SURVEY

Year	Members	Sunday School	Congregational Expense	Benevolences
1929	60	16	$1,326	$201
1930	63	63	1,528	400
1931	62	71	1,160	298
1932	60	78	1,334	331
1933	60	65	1,318	100
1934	69	80	1,288	238
1935	81	65	1,152	350
1936	82	85	760	161
1937	81	74	571	89
1938	83	85	693	100
1939	85	70	1,109	96
1940	82	70	900	249
1941	84	69	950	123
1942	84	51	895	202
1943	103	62	668	207
1944	98	37	1,042	262
1945	89	60	825	168
1946	93	51	850	146
1947	93	55	1,199	505
1948	89	62	1,079	537
1949	84	49	1,929	518
1950	87	45	2,535	1,602
1951	78	51	4,360	532
1952	81	55	3,700	1,100
1953	79	50	4,582	379

causes. Charted on a graph, these increases will usually appear rather outstanding during the last ten years. It is necessary to remember that the entire financial structure of our present-day economy has changed completely. From the low of depression days to the high of the last few years, incomes have increased exceptionally. In spite of the inflationary spiral which has resulted from the devaluation of the dollar, the buying power of rural people remains about two hundred per cent what it was during the depression. With this in mind, the upswing of financial support in the church takes on quite a different appearance.

Every pastor of a rural church is interested in establishing the geographical area of his community. This geographical community will, to a great extent, determine the outreach to which his congregation will be limited. With some communities it is not difficult to find this geographical area. A river may border one side, and hills or swamp or some other natural barrier the other, so that without research the extent of the community can readily be determined. Sociologists have for many years pointed out the fact that it is uncommon and unnatural for people to cross natural barriers from one geographical area to another in seeking a church home. Some very interesting studies have been made showing that even a railroad track may constitute such a barrier.

One of the tools in establishing community boundaries is a plat map. Township and county plat maps are obtainable from various sources. They may be purchased in a county assessor's office. Frequently, the predominant farmers' organization in the area will have them on sale. The state and county highway commissions also have these maps. Usually, the county plat map is taken in segments, the size of a township. Upon the township map is platted each farm. The locations of the buildings are indicated on the farm and the name of the owner given. A map of this kind can be of invaluable service to the pastor. If the church is located in a town, the plat map of the town may be obtained from the mayor's office. Frequently it is necessary to copy the map because only one master map has been made.

After the pastor has obtained a plat map, he should go to the school superintendent, asking him to indicate on the map the extreme geographical locations from which his students come. The map may then be taken to the banker to have him indicate the widest circle from which the bank receives its patronage. The same should be done with a grocer and other representative businessmen. The pastor will then locate his parishioners on the map and draw a circle including these. This circle contrasted with the others will indicate whether the community influence of the church is as extensive as that of other services in the area.

The pastor of the Cross Roads Federated Church, after getting this information, found that the community in which his church functioned was limited to the east because of a river that was two and a half miles from the village. Toward the south the community circle of the church coincided with that of the other services of the village, but toward both the west and the north it fell far short. This pointed out to him that he would need to determine why his church had little or no influence in these two directions.

Another source of information, which has been referred to before in this book, is the United States census. A wealth of information about the community in which the church is functioning can be gathered from this publication.

The pastor can find access to the census materials in the nearest county seat town library. Most of these libraries are depositories for the census, and as the Government Printing Office completes them, the volumes are sent to these depositories. If the pastor is located near a college library, he will certainly find the material catalogued there. Even the small colleges receive these publications.

The volumes that can be most useful are entitled *Population — General Characteristics*. These volumes break down the population to the town and township levels. They give the number of people in every age bracket from 0–4 years to those above 75. By simple research, the pastor can contrast the various age groups by ten-year periods from 1910 to 1950. This will show him an over-all trend of population in his own community. Another valuable piece of information that these volumes of the United States census contain deals with the stability of population in the area. The percentage of people who move each year has been worked out. There are many other bits of information which the pastor interested in research may glean about his locality. The condition of the housing units, the amount of products raised, the chief businesses and industries in the area, and many other helpful facts may be found. The pastor is limited only by the time he wishes to spend in this research.

For the community in which the Cross Roads Federated Church was located the United States census revealed the following data.

Table 5 immediately reveals that the Cross Roads Federated Church was working in an area with a declining population except

Table 5

TOTAL POPULATION IN AREA FOR 40 YEARS

Year	Population
1910	1,841
1920	1,776
1930	1,690
1940	1,601
1950	1,531

Table 6

1930 AND 1950 POPULATION IN

VARIOUS AGE GROUPS CONTRASTED

Age	Number in 1930	Percentage of Total	Number in 1950	Percentage of Total
0-4	155	9.2	155	10.1
5-9	144	8.5	132	8.6
10-14	152	9.	122	8.
15-19	161	9.5	115	7.5
20-24	144	8.5	109	7.1
25-29	122	7.2	92	6.
30-34	118	7.	110	7.2
35-39	106	6.3	97	6.3
40-44	103	6.1	95	6.2
45-49	105	6.2	95	6.2
50-54	101	6.	95	6.2
55-59	78	4.6	72	4.7
60-64	68	4.	86	5.6
65	134	7.9	158	10.3

from 1910 to 1930, when there was an increase; following 1930 the decline has been greater than the increase of the prior twenty years. This of course means that the three churches functioning in the immediate area have less people to work with than they had twenty years ago; consequently a goal toward church growth appears limited or impossible.

Table 6 indicates three factors of immediate importance to this church. There is a marked decrease in the number of children up to nine years of age. There has been an even larger decrease in the number of youth fifteen to nineteen years of age. There are considerably more people above sixty years than there were in 1930.

The fourth source of information (by all means the most important) is the people themselves. House-to-house surveys are by no means a new technique. They have been made for many years to gather all sorts of information. Manufacturers have used this technique to determine how popular their products were. The church has used this technique during the past twenty or thirty years. A house-to-house survey can be exceedingly useful when it is not made just as an end in itself. The writer remembers with a great deal of glee one of his experiences with such a survey. He had been asked to study a certain growing section of a medium-sized Midwestern city for the purpose of determining whether a new church should be started. When he first came into town, he spoke to the pastors of the established churches. They immediately informed him that a house-to-house survey had been made some six months prior to that date. He asked to see that survey and its analysis, but none of the pastors was able to direct him to the location of the schedules filled out in the survey. One pastor said, "It was one of the best religious surveys I have ever had a hand in making; we covered a very high percentage of the town." In spite of the enthusiasm no analysis had been made and the schedules had apparently disappeared. Several days later the writer was in a barbershop. The barber, passing the time of day, asked him his business. He informed the barber that he was interested in making a survey for church purposes. The barber showed a great deal of interest, indicating that his wife had worked for weeks upon the survey that had been made six months before. The writer then said that he had been looking for the schedules with the analysis of the survey, but no one seemed to know where they were to be found. The barber laughed and said, "They are in pasteboard boxes under the bed in our spare bedroom." It was there that the writer finally located the schedules. Too often after a careful survey has been completed, no actual use is made of the results. Consequently, people become impatient with this type of study and will resent another survey.

On the other hand, the information gathered in a survey can be of great help if rightly utilized and carefully analyzed.

The first thing that should be done when a religious house-to-house survey is being contemplated is to contact through the county or local ministerial organization all the pastors working in the area that is to be studied. Winning their confidence and co-operation will, to a large extent, determine the success or failure of the survey. The impact of a united effort is always greater than the impression left by one man and his church doing the work alone. Community or county-wide publicity can much more readily be gained from the newspapers on the co-operative basis. Business and secular organizations as well as church groups will frequently work together. The techniques of administering the survey will be the same whether the one church does it or a co-operating group. The items of information that are to be gathered must first be agreed upon. One of the very best schedules that has been worked out for this purpose was developed by the Iowa Christian Rural Fellowship in 1946. With this schedule almost half of the State of Iowa was contacted, family by family. The schedule is reproduced on page 65.

The schedule opposite contains three types of information. The first section, items 1 to 8, deals with the location and stability of the family interviewed. Section 9 to 14 deals with the religious affiliation of the family. Items 15 and 16 deal with economic and social aspects.

Organization of a Religious Census

In another section of this book the author has stated that the most complete census can best be accomplished with the co-operation of all the churches in the community. However, it is also possible to take a thoroughly accurate census with several churches dissenting. A church working alone has been known to make a fairly accurate

Iowa Religious Census

County________ Interviewer and Date________

1. Family Name________ 2. Street address or R. D. No.________

3. Post Office________ 4. Township________ 5. Section No.________

6. Resident of this community since________ 7. Resident of this farm since________ 8. Home Owner or Renter________

Names of Members of Household living at home	13. Age	14. CHURCH AFFILIATION (a) Member of What Church?	(b) Church Location	(c) Local Church Preference	(d) Attendance Church	(d) Attendance S. S.	15. INDUSTRY AND OCCUPATION					
9. Head												
10. Wife												
							16. YOUTH AFFILIATIONS					
11. Children							Church Y. org.	4-H Club	Scouts C. F.	Other	School Attendance	Employed
(a)												
(b)												
(c)												
(d)												
(e)												
12. Others in Household												
(a)												
(b)												
(c)												

17. REMARKS________

study. In any case, the following procedure, which is based upon most churches' co-operating, should be followed in whole or in part.

The co-operating bodies should first determine the geographical extent or area which the census is to cover. This geographical area may be determined in part by a study of the community as described earlier in the chapter.

The committee will then decide upon a definite period of time. If the area covered is large and more than 2,000 families are to be contacted, it may be best to set from three days to a week. Usually the canvassers will gather at a central location on a Sunday afternoon and after a short service of dedication will enter upon their job, to return a week later with full results.

The third step is the development of a good program of publicity. The editors of the weekly or daily newspapers in the area either should be present at the early planning stage or should receive careful reports so that four major statements concerning the census may appear in their publications: (1) a preliminary report concerning the decision to make a survey; (2) a report on the date and the geographical area to be covered, with a request for people to co-operate with the interviewers; (3) a listing of the interviewers with another plea for co-operation, just before the census is taken; (4) a report on the results.

The area to be covered should be cut up into segments small enough for each team to cover without a great expenditure of time. The plat maps which have been acquired are cut into segments as described above. Each segment is pasted on the worker's envelope. In this envelope is a sheet of instructions and sufficient schedules to cover the people living in the assigned area.

The co-operating committee through its organizations and agencies makes an appeal to its constituency for volunteer workers. There should be sufficient workers so that each team will need to contact from 15 to 20 families in the country, and 20 to 30 families in the town. It is possible in a strictly urban area where entire apartment houses are covered for the team to contact more.

About two days before the start of the survey, all workers should gather for a two-hour period of instruction. At this time sample schedules should be placed in the hands of each team. The instructor should carefully go through the schedule with all workers, actually interviewing a family (one of the workers may volunteer), so that the procedure may be carefully watched by the group. The instructor should be prepared to answer all questions pertaining to the schedule and the program. At the end of this carefully planned period of instruction, the team assignments should be made and the workers' envelopes handed out. The period of time assigned for actual house-to-house contacts should be utilized for that purpose. All teams must complete their interviews within the time limit. If the interviews are allowed to extend beyond the assigned time limits, the interest of both workers and those to be interviewed wanes.

At a time which has been predetermined all teams return to a central location to bring in their results. Two or three hours of an afternoon or evening may be assigned to this step.

The people in charge of the survey will next tabulate and chart the results, which will be available to all the churches and organizations co-operating. The follow-up, which naturally ought to take place, will be as successful only as the determined efforts of those interested.

A letter expressing appreciation for services rendered should be sent to each team that co-operated in the canvass.

Explanation of Religious Schedule

Item 1. Under " Family Name " the name of the husband is given. However, in case the widow is the head of the family, her name would appear.

Item 2. It is important that the street address or rural delivery number be included.

Item 3. Post office at which the family receives its mail.

Items 4 and 5. For location of a family it is quite important that both the township and section number be given if the family live in the country. If they live in town, items 4 and 5 may be ignored.

Items 6 to 8. These three items deal directly with the stability of the family in relationship to the community. It is very important that the interviewers get this information. From many surveys and studies that have been made it has been learned that homeowners support the church with attendance and finances to a greater degree than renters. Church attendance is also affected by the number of years that a family has lived in a community. People who move almost every year are not likely to have active membership in any church.

Item 9. As stated under item 1, the head of the house is usually the husband; however, there are households in which a widow, a brother, a sister, or even an older child, may be considered the head of the home. This name should then appear in item 9.

Item 10. This item is filled out only if item 9 is the husband.

Item 11. The names of the children at home should appear in chronological order from the oldest to the youngest. In case there are more than five children, an additional line may be drawn on the schedule.

Item 12. Frequently there are other members in the household, such as an aunt, grandfather or grandmother, a hired man who makes his home with the family, children of other parents, etc. These should appear in column 12.

Item 13. This column, entitled "Age," is quite important. Many interviewers have experienced difficulty in getting the age of the wife. Usually the husband is willing to give his. If there appears to be any reticence on the part of the interviewed, the census taker may guess and put an approximate age in the column. It is, however, important that the ages of the children be quite accurate; few families object to giving these.

Item 14. This item should give the name of the church to which the person interviewed belongs. Column b should give the specific location of that church. Frequently a and b are different from column c. A person may be a member of the First Lutheran Church of Fox River, Indiana, but may be living in Hilldale, Missouri, attending the Zion Lutheran Church. Column c consequently should give the name of the local church preferred. If c is the same as a, c should remain blank.

In the two columns under d the attendance at church and Sunday school are indicated; that is, the interviewed is asked whether he attends church regularly. If he says yes, it is so indicated on the schedule. The same is true of Sunday school. Definite answers, either yes or no, should be given for all members of the family. If the question is raised, "What is meant by regular attendance?," the interviewer should be ready to explain. The co-operating committee in this census is the body that ought to determine what regular attendance means for its community. In some communities this is set at twice a month. Others have even accepted once a month as regular attendance.

Item 15. The occupation of the head of the house usually appears here. It is true that in many cases both husband and wife work. If this is the case, both may be given.

Item 16. There are six columns under "Youth Affiliations," which can be very helpful to the pastor in determining his relationship to the church and to his young people. In the first column under "16" it should be stated whether the children belong to some youth organization besides the Sunday school. Usually the name of the organization appears. Column 2 is specifically aimed at rural boys and girls — do they belong to a 4-H club? Column 3 fits into the program of town boys and girls — are they members of boy or girl scout organizations? In the fourth column the name of other organizations to which they belong may be written. The fifth column, entitled "School Attendance," should be answered by inserting the grade in school in which the child is enrolled. For example, 10th. The final column under "Youth Affiliations" should point out whether the person is employed, if not in school; or if he is in school, does he have part-time employment?

Item 17. The interviewer may comment concerning any items that may not be self-explanatory.

The three churches functioning in the area in which the Cross Roads Federated Church was located made a house-to-house survey. After it had been completed and carefully analyzed, they found the information in Tables 7 and 8, page 70.

The pastor of the Federated Church and a committee representing the congregation met to discuss the information that had been gathered thus far. They found from the study on community boundaries that their church was limited in two areas. The census revealed that the community was declining in population and that young people left the area when they were between the ages of 15 and 29. An increased number of old people was noted in the community. The greatest challenge to the group, however, came from

Table 7

AFFILIATION OF PEOPLE CONTACTED

Protestant	644
Roman Catholic	327
No Church Affiliation	433

Table 8

NUMBER OF PEOPLE CLAIMING CHURCH MEMBERSHIP

Head of House	285
Wife	293
Under 15 Years	196
15-19 Years	93
20-29 Years	37
Others	71

the house-to-house census: 126 families, or almost one third of the population, were unchurched. Although the total population was declining, apparently there was hope for growth within the area. Most of these unchurched people lived in the community area not covered by the church.

The committee recognized that the church needed to develop a plan: (1) to strengthen the services to the larger number of little children in the area, (2) to co-operate with other organizations and agencies in attracting more of the young people to business and farms within the community, (3) to start a program that would fit the needs of the rapidly growing number of older people in the area, (4) to organize an intensive campaign among the unchurched in the area.

Although the committee of the Cross Roads Federated Church realized that the church could never expect to become numerically a large one, it could at least increase considerably in size and could render a much more significant contribution to the total life of the community.

Any pastor who is vitally interested in people and in his church can follow the suggestions given in this chapter. Careful planning based upon known needs and information will usually result in greater services rendered to the people and the community. The final result will be a greatly strengthened church.

Chapter 6

SETTING UP GOALS

THE ACTUAL REASON for analyzing and studying the background of a parish, its constituency and its potential, is not merely the acquisition of factual material but rather that consistent, intelligent programing can be developed. In light of the materials that are thus gathered, goals for achievement should next be set up. Most aggressive organizations and institutions set up achievement goals for which to strive at the beginning of regular time cycles. Sometimes these are set up at the beginning of each year; again they may be in cycles of three or five years. Public education in recent years has definitely pioneered in this area. In most states very little planning had been accomplished and very little change of legislation had been made in the public school systems from the early pioneer period to very recent times. However, during the past ten or fifteen years, most states have recognized the inadequacy of the old educational program. Committees were set up to analyze trends and study the potentials so that new achievement goals might be developed. In most cases these goals were not set up for one year, but rather for a period of years, sometimes covering an entire decade. The Middle Western states have been especially successful in this planning.

Churches have been very slow to adopt achievement goals. It is true that denominations and interdenominational agencies have developed check sheets which have been suggested to local churches. However, in most cases, these have not been adopted on the local level; or, if they have, only lip service has been done to them. One of the earliest achievement goals which appeared as a sort of check sheet was developed by Dr. W. H. Stacy, of Iowa State College. Since that time other denominational and interdenominational agencies have developed such check sheets. In the Christian Rural Fellowship organizations of both the Methodist and Presbyterian Churches, such sheets have been printed and given quite wide distribution.

The setting up of achievement goals for a local church must be distinguished from the programing which should also take place. Programing implements the achievement of the goal. Consequently before this work can be done, goals must be developed. At the present time in denominations and local churches programing has been developed to a rather high degree. It has been done, however, without a systematic and regular acceptance of goals to be achieved. Much of the programing is adopted by local churches because of pressure which denominational officials exert upon them. The consequence of such action has shown itself again and again in the rather halfhearted attempts on the part of the laity to carry into action the suggested programs. In a democratic society, whether the organization is a church, a school, or a lodge, it becomes imperative that the people themselves set up the achievement goals. These should result from their own study of needs and goals for accomplishment. Consequently, goals that are not the result of indigenous planning can at best be used only as guides and should never be adopted totally as a standard for achievement of the local group.

The pastor of the local church in seeking to set up achievement goals for his congregation should not act alone. A committee consisting of representatives of each organization of the church and several members at large should meet at frequent intervals to examine the particular needs as well as the potential of the church. There are five areas that should come under special attention in the development of these goals. These are spiritual, social and recreational, numerical and material, outreach, and service. Because of poor planning many churches entirely omit one or several of these areas of achievement. Pastors who have special training in one of these will emphasize that one and neglect another. For these and other reasons a well-rounded program is frequently lacking in the rural church.

Spiritual Goals

Under the stress that the present-day society places upon the church, its major sphere of activity is frequently subordinated. This becomes particularly noticeable when goals for achievement are being followed. Under a welter of activity the spiritual purposes of the Christian church sometimes become lost. Yet traditionally the primary and predominant emphases of the church have always been in the spiritual realm. To cause men to realize their spiritual relationship to the Supreme Being and to give opportunity for men to develop that relationship has always been the first obligation of the Christian church. Consequently, this is the first area in which goals ought to be set. Again, because it is both impractical and impossible to present an exact outline for all local churches, the author proposes to make some general suggestions which local committees must interpret and develop to fit their own situations.

Preaching has been for many years the one universally accepted mode for the development of the spiritual welfare of the people. Professors of homiletics have long taught that there are various types of sermons that fill the needs of people. The local church should set up for its pastor certain goals for his preaching program. Many pastors have become known for their one-sided program. It may be that one pastor preaches almost exclusively topical sermons dealing with the political and economic situations pertaining to his time. Another pastor may preach exclusively decision-demanding evangelistic sermons. In order to help people not only to come alive in the spiritual realm, but also to grow, preaching goals should be set up to cover all aspects of life. The pastor should consider as a minimum goal the following areas of preaching: (1) expository, using the Scriptures as his textbook; (2) evangelistic, in which he appeals to his hearers for a decision; (3) topical, in which he interprets the meaning of the contemporary events to people who are trying to live a Christian life; (4) doctrinal, in which the pastor expounds to his people the major emphasis to which his particular faith group adheres.

The continual repetition of only one of these emphases is likely to leave the constituents of the church spiritually starved. An inclusive preaching program will also keep the pastor alert. He will need to know current events as well as to continue his study of the Scriptures and good literature.

To enlist every family of the local church in home devotions needs also to be set as a minimum goal. Many helps are now available, both denominational and nondenominational. The real strength of spiritual well-being is not developed in the Sunday service at the church alone. The home should again, as it has done in the past, play a major role in this area of responsibility.

It can readily be seen that many other areas in the work of the church can be aimed at the spiritual welfare of the people. From the choir to the Christian education program, influences that affect the spiritual life of the people can be traced. Consequently, any goals that are set up in these areas must also be considered as partially spiritual.

Directed pastoral calling, with major emphasis on the spiritual welfare of the people visited, becomes an important tool in the development of this aspect of life. As can easily be surmised, the goals to strive for in this activity are largely determined by the conduct and attitude of the pastor. In recent years another implement has been emphasized: the activity of lay visitation. When teams of laymen call from home to home to press upon the families the need for a deepening spiritual experience, actual progress in the life of the church as a unit can be noted.

Social and Recreational Goals

As is often stressed, yet frequently misunderstood, much of the experience of man lies in the social and recreational fields. For many years the church has either ignored or denied its responsibility in each of these areas. It has been impossible, however, for the church to draw itself completely aside from the social influence because whenever people meet together in a common cause, sit together in worship, and strive together to support a church, a social need is being met. The walking together to church, the discussion after services, the family activity in preparing for church—all these are actually a part of the total social experience of men. They may even include a recreational experience. In recent years it has become increasingly evident that in our complex society the church plays an ever-developing role of importance in these fields. A committee that studies the over-all goals toward which the local church should strive must of necessity face this one. In many sections where the church is the one remaining agency that draws families together in neighborhood experience, the social responsibility must be met almost entirely by this institution. Consequently, the committee that sets up goals should realistically face this responsibility.

However, it is also noteworthy that other organizations within the community furnish a social experience for their constituents. Service clubs, farmers' organizations, lodges, schools, and many others help to bring a total social and recreational experience to those involved. In setting up achievement goals, the committee whose responsibility it has become must recognize this factor and in recognizing it must also give room to other organizations. If not, open competition will eventually develop into conflict, and the church, which should bring harmony and peace to a community, will be responsible for disharmony and fragmentation.

Numerical and Material Goals

Too often the total basis of judgment on the adequacy of the local church, its effectiveness and its worth, is placed entirely upon its material and numeric growth. Whether the congregation has grown numerically seems more important than whether it has grown spiritually. Whether the church has made major structural improvements becomes a higher basis of judgment than whether it has sent missionaries from its constituents into needy parts of the world. Whether the Sunday school increased by at least 10 per cent each year appears more important than whether the members of the school have grown in knowledge of the gospel and its application in Christian ethics.

Recently this was clearly shown by the following example. A pastor from an adjoining state came to the office of the writer. He was deeply perturbed. After spending a great deal of time discussing the trivialities of the day, he finally came to the purpose of his journey. He was of the opinion that he should have the opportunity to move to a new location. For almost nine years he had been the faithful pastor of a rural congregation. His ability and sincerity were not to be questioned. During the first five years of his pastorate a net gain in membership, Sunday school enrollment, and finances could be reported. However, during the last four years, a gradual deterioration had set in. A net loss of 7 per cent in both Sunday school and church enrollment was evident. People in the local church as well as those in his state denominational body were of the opinion that he had ended his productive years in that location and that his effectiveness had diminished to a point where it might be helpful to the congregation if he should leave. Although he was ready to consider a new charge, he felt very unhappy and somewhat frustrated by this turn of events. The writer realized that if he moved to another location without facing the real cause for the decline in his church, his over-all effectiveness might be impaired. After carefully inquiring into the program of the church, the writer suggested that after two weeks the pastor should come to see him again. The man appreciated this gesture, and agreed to return. During these two weeks, the writer carefully made a sociological study of the county, township, and village in which the church was located. A thirty-year survey indicated that, as has been the case in many rural areas, the population was dwindling. There were 13 per cent less people in the area than had been there a decade before. There were 11 per cent less children enrolled in the public school than had been ten years earlier. The younger families and the young people were moving out of the county into a metropolitan area some sixty miles distant. The pastor who had been working against these difficulties and odds was not losing his grip. In fact, both his church membership and Sunday school enrollment had dwindled by only 7 per cent. This, contrasted to the over-all 13 per cent loss of population and 11 per cent loss of school population, indicated that he had gained a net of 6 per cent in the church and 4 per cent in the Sunday school. The writer immediately sent a letter to the pastor, asking that when he returned, he should bring with him an outstanding lay leader of his congregation. The pastor agreed with reluctance. When the lay leader and the pastor saw the graphs and tables that had been prepared, they were amazed. The lay leader looked at his pastor with new affection. He asked for the tables and charts and took them back to the congregation. Today that pastor is still actively engaged in the same community, with his effectiveness unchallenged and unquestioned.

This indicates the misjudgments that can result from an over-emphasis on numeric increase. It goes without question that the Christian church ought to increase in size, that the outreach of the local church ought to be continued, and that people who are not affiliated with a church ought to be brought under its influence. However, in setting up goals, the sociological conditions in the area must be brought into focus. In the cutover areas of Wisconsin which are steadily losing population it would be ridiculous to challenge a congregation with a percentage increase at the same rate that a congregation in the fast-growing areas just outside of Madison should be challenged. Only with the information at hand that can be acquired from the studies suggested in Chapter 5 can a local church committee most intelligently develop numeric and material goals.

There is no doubt that many church buildings need to be expanded and that adequate education plants must be built. However, the fact that a large number of churches are engaged in building should not determine that all churches need be thus engaged. Again in this area, the committee on goals must be careful in analyzing the local needs not only on the basis of the immediate period but also on the basis of the situation that will pertain in another decade.

Financial stewardship is another part of material gain. This area frequently becomes the easiest in which to make suggested increased goals. That Christian people today have not adequately met the challenge of stewardship goes without question and anything that can be done to raise stewardship responsibility certainly ought to be commended. However, it is not amiss to point out that financial increase in goals must be accompanied by an adequate stewardship education program. Just to attempt to raise financial goals by persuasion and pressure without achieving the willingness of spirit actually will be detrimental to the over-all achievement goals in any congregation.

Outreach Goals

Years ago when the writer was a lad, he saw a picture in one of the Church papers to which his father subscribed, of an artist's conception of a dead church. To most people today the picture is a familiar one. Cathedral doors with a lofty and beautiful Gothic arch outlining them, depicting a beautiful edifice, had at the side of the door the mission benevolence box with a slot in the top for money. A spider had woven its web across the top of the box, thus making it apparent that this function of the church had long been unused. When the church's outreach is withheld, the congregation is spiritually dead. This is as true today as it was a score of years ago. In order to keep spiritually alive and alert, the local congregation must continue to consider others. Thus, when the committee develops goals for achievement, this phase of the work of the church should come in for its share of emphasis. The financial program is an important part. To support the missionary outreach of the denomination is mandatory for large and small churches alike. The ideal goal for which to strive should be fifty cents of every dollar to missions and outreach. However, there are many limiting factors that must be considered by the committee. The small church that already carries a heavy load cannot be expected to contribute the same high proportion that a large congregation can achieve. Nevertheless, even churches receiving mission aid ought to strive for goals that require them to give a portion of their income to others.

There is another side to the outreach program that is frequently neglected. It is the channeling of young people into missionary and regular church professions. Missionaries and pastors as well as other church leaders must come from some source. Many churches are parasitical. They constantly consume leadership without ever contributing. Statistically, every congregation should contribute at least one young person every twenty-five years to this cause. This will merely replace the personnel that the church consumes. Recruiting young people for Christian service must become part of the outreach goals of the congregation.

The third segment of outreach on the local church level is the members' responsibility for the pagans and nonmembers within the church community. Goals should be presented that will challenge the members to reach out within the community to the unchurched neighbors and friends.

Service Goals

It has frequently been stated that the largest source of community leadership has its training in the Christian church. There can be little argument against the fact that the morals of a community are largely determined by the quality and the ethics of the leaders functioning in the area. The church's greatest contribution to the community is not made by mass intervention, by pulpit condemnation, or even by a congregation withdrawing itself from the surrounding life. The greatest contribution is made by the constant flow of Christian people into the many complex activities of the community. Frequently a complaint is made by leaders in the local church that the 4-H clubs, scouts, service organizations, Red Cross, farmers' organizations, and others absorb so much of the time of the church's constituent membership that it becomes difficult to find sufficient leadership to carry on the work of the congregation. Although on the surface this often-repeated complaint appears legitimate, it may also be a blessing in disguise. It is in this way that the Christian impact can best be made on the affairs of men. To prepare consecrated Christians for leadership and then to inject that leadership into community affairs is a very desirable process. The church's committee that is interested in a series of attainable goals should constantly be aware of this major contribution which the church by the very nature of its organization ought to make.

On a smaller scale this matter of Christian service deals not only with the leadership in the church but also with every member. The ultimate goal of achievement for which the committee should strive is the opportunity for every member, young or old, to be of service. This service can be within the local church, a smaller organization, community affairs, or on a much wider basis.

A decade or two ago the group that was usually neglected within the church was the young people. During the past fifteen years, great strides forward have been made in opening up avenues of service for youth. The new group that should come to the attention of every goal-developing committee is now to be found among the older generation; the average life span of people has been increased amazingly. Large numbers of men and women who have stepped out of income-producing and time-consuming activities now are unchallenged in the church. Restlessness, frustration, and unhappiness result. Today no goal-setting committee dare ignore this group. With mature judgment, adequate time, and able skills, when challenged by sufficiently important goals this large group will be able to make a real contribution through the services that it can render.

Under these five headings achievement goals for any local congregation can be developed. The setting up of goals is only preliminary to the actual program development. Pastors frequently see the opportunity for goal planning; they succeed in developing great enthusiasm in the congregation during the period of discussing goals. After these have been set up they fail to implement the achievement by an actual program that can be developed. The result is a gradual cooling of enthusiasm on the part of the people. After such an experience it becomes doubly difficult to set up any kind of workable program.

Chapter 7

DEVELOPING THE PROGRAM AND CHECKING RESULTS

THUS FAR this book has dealt with the background of the people with whom the rural church works. It has pointed out the many influences that have helped to develop our American rural civilization. The second step was to show sociological, economic, and educational factors which also have their bearing upon the total program of the church. The third step in the approach to this book was to show how over-all goals need to be kept in mind by church workers. Now, the actual programing, or the techniques by which goals are achieved, must be considered.

Artificial programing has in recent years been the order of the day. Following the depression, many such programs set up by so-called "brain trusters" were handed down to the people. So long as these programs were implemented by subsidies from the outside, they seemed to flourish. As soon as these subsidies were withdrawn, many of them failed. This failure was largely due to the fact that the program itself was not tailor-made to the situation.

At frequent intervals the Christian churches go through similar experiences. Programing in stereotpye form is frequently handed down to the local congregation without due consideration of the local factors that pertain. When these programs are accepted without adaptation, they often fail. We must hasten to add that most denominational boards and officials that are involved in the development of programs do not expect the local church to accept their program without adaptation. The ingenuity of local leadership in remaking a handed-down program is largely responsible for its success on the local level. Programing from the denominational level except in most general terms would be abandoned if local churches were more willing to make very careful and minute plans in developing the over-all denominational goals. It is because the local church with its leadership has not done this that so much of the programing is now placed in the hands of boards and denominational bodies. It is rather difficult to explain the reasons that local churches neglect their own programing. It may be that the traditional type of general church work that has been handed down from generation to generation seems sufficient to local leaders. It may also be that local leadership lacks initiative and imagination.

The basis for American democracy has always been strongly entrenched in the hands of local leadership. As our democracy has grown older, this local leadership has surrendered this prerogative to national and professional leadership outside of the community. The last twenty years have increasingly been marked by this trend. It may be that the local agencies and institutions affected by this national trend have permitted these to permeate their own organizations. In spite of trends it remains true that the most effective programing is the kind that is developed and put into action by local people with their own organizations.

The pastor of the local church remains the key to good planning. His leadership, which must always be positive and never dictatorial, can do much in the enactment of a strong program. He needs to remember two major facts:

1. That a program developed and enforced by himself alone will largely be built around his personality. Upon his removal to another area, it will go "by the board." Consequently the pastor should involve as many of his people both in places of important leadership as well as in the actual enactment as he possibly can. The very best church program is one in which every member feels he has a necessary part.

2. That the membership of the local church frequently has not had training and direction to carry out a well-planned church program. Consequently, it becomes his task through leadership training schools to develop lay leadership to such an extent that if

he is called away before the program has been completed, there will be little or no interruption in its completion.

What Shall the Program Be?

The pastor with his planning committee who has followed the suggestions in the preceding chapters will have a mass of information at hand. He will know the immediate needs of his community and will also have recognized the trends of population and other factors. In his relationship to his denomination he will also have received the general suggested program for his church which has been planned to direct over-all denominational progress. With all this material in hand he can best plot the program on the local level. He will know what needs to be eliminated. For example, let us assume that his denomination has sent out material suggesting that the local church carry on a careful program of family visitation in the rapidly developing suburbs or segments of the town. However, he and his church are located in an area from which people are moving rather than one to which people go. Since there are no new suburbs or new village segments, this portion of the program could not be implemented in his area. On the other hand, his denomination also proposes that a crusade be undertaken to contact every boy and girl in behalf of the church school educational program. In contrasting the total enrollment of church schools in his area to the public school population, the pastor finds that for every two pupils in the public school there is only one in the church school. Part of his local program therefore would be to contact all families with children for the purpose of recruiting scholars for the church school. Gradually in this way the pastor will go through the entire denominational program to see how much can be integrated in the local scene.

After he has done this he will carefully scan the needs of his community and his church in the light of the materials that he has gathered. Certain needs that can best be met through an organized program may be uncovered from this study. For example, although his denomination has not emphasized the integration of old people into the program of the church, he has many retired folks who have moved into the village in which his church is located. He will immediately sense the necessity of giving these folks an essential activity within the church. Consequently his program will include not only the suggestions on the denominational level but also the actual needs on the local level.

For anyone to outline a suggested program that might be adopted in all rural churches would be impossible. In other words, the program that the local pastor develops will be the one which most nearly meets all the needs of his local people, including the general needs of his denomination. Questions will naturally arise in the mind of the pastor in the development of such an all-inclusive plan. For example, a village that was twenty-four miles from the nearest resident doctor had a great need for medical service. The village itself did not have the leadership through which these services might be obtained. For more than a year the local pastor struggled within himself to determine whether it would be legitimate for him to include as part of the programing of his church the obtaining of medical services for the community. In his second year he felt that he and his church must take action. A committee was set up, of which he was chairman because there did not seem to be adequate leadership available otherwise. Subscriptions were taken from people of his church as well as from others within the community, a house and office were obtained, a young doctor was contacted and guaranteed a minimum salary. As a result, the village now has medical services. A permanent committee has been appointed to continue this relationship. Now that more leadership has been made available, the pastor has stepped out of the immediate picture.

How Shall the Program Be Enacted?

It is frequently said by outstanding community leaders that a few of the people do all the work, or "If you want a thing done, ask Mr. So-and-So to do it; he is responsible for most everything and somehow gets it done." This is a questionable trap into which many leaders fall. There is no doubt that certain people have a great deal of natural ability and upon them are thrust all areas of community and church leadership. Usually this is done because the church wishes to get the job completed with the greatest dispatch and the least worry. It can readily be seen that only a limited number of the church's constituency are thus made responsible for the ongoing programing.

Some years ago hundreds of young people who were members of the Iowa Rural Young People's Assembly were contacted in a survey concerning church relationship. One of the questions that was asked them had to do with the responsibilities that were placed on their shoulders from the entire program of their home church. Many of their answers were to the effect that no responsibility was given them, or in case some responsibility was placed upon them, it was of an insignificant nature. A young woman who taught school for several years appended a letter to her survey schedule. In it she voiced the feeling of many young people. She stated that responsibilities that were given to youth by the official church board were usually so insignificant that they meant nothing to the continuing life of the church. She contended that if the church expected young people to be loyal and gradually take over their appointed place in a congregation, the responsibilities handed to them must be more than a "sop."

The ways of democracy are slow. They depend upon, not merely a few leaders, but all citizens involved. The responsibility of a democratic society lies, not upon a few, but upon all. This principle is just as true in the church. The program of the church with its enactment belongs, not to a few, but to all. The future and progress of the church is not the responsibility merely of the preacher and his board, but of every member, including those enrolled in the Sunday school, the youth organizations, and the home department. Churches that show a phenomenal amount of success in a community are usually those that have every member busy at work in needed parts of the program.

Let us apply this principle to some actual situations.

Situation 1. This church is located in a village serving both village and country people. Farmers, as they retire from the land, move into the village. There are many older people in the area as a consequence. In the general pastoral visitation program which the minister has conducted, he has heard the frequent complaint from these older people that they are isolated from outside activities and have become lonesome. On the other hand the pastor has also felt the frustration that comes to people who have been active all their lives and now have retirement thrust upon them. Realizing that it was not possible for him to visit the shut-ins frequently enough or to be with those who felt frustrated, he inaugurated a program by which the older people who were healthy were made responsible for the visitation of a certain number of shut-ins each month. Thus the pastor has recognized two needs and met them both by a process of programing which gave to those who visited a feeling that they were no longer forgotten.

Situation 2. The over-all denominational program adopted for a given year included plans for every local church to carry out a schedule of evangelism and outreach. It was up to the local church to determine just how this should be enacted. Some pastors recognized the program in general. Preaching evangelistic sermons once a month, asking for a prospect list from the congregation, visiting the families thus listed, and writing letters to the indifferent became the order of the day. Other pastors considered this an overall challenge which should occupy every member of the congregation so far as possible. First, a survey was carried out, sponsored by the young married couples' organization. Second, a committee of the men's club analyzed the survey. Third, from the congregation as a whole, visitation teams were organized and two weeks of intensive lay visitation evangelism were conducted. Members of the young people's organization were made responsible for bringing boys and girls into the church school and to the young people's organization. The old people were appointed to call upon other old couples that had drifted from the church. Sunday school teachers were asked to place special emphasis on the claims of Christ to each church school pupil. A family night to which all families that had been contacted were invited was held at the church. This was the responsibility of the women's organization. Every organization of the church was given a place of responsibility in this evangelistic outreach drive.

Situation 3. It sometimes becomes evident in the life of the church that one organization or another is largely neglected so far as responsible activities are concerned. In this programing it is not always possible for the entire church to carry some segment of the same program emphasis. Sometimes such an emphasis can best be completed by a single organization. In this particular community, there was exceedingly strong competition for the time of the people. The school with its athletic events and the church were frequently in conflict. Other social organizations were also making a strong bid for the time of the people. A young mothers' club was solicited for the job of bringing order out of chaos. This club had had little opportunity to conduct any major emphasis in church work — small children occupied most of their time. This, however, was a challenge that they could accept because most of the work could be conducted by telephone after a preliminary meeting or two. Leaders of every major organization in the village and surrounding territory were called together. A community calendar was suggested. Certain nights were set aside for school activities. One night besides Sunday was set aside for church activities; one night was set aside as home night; social and service organizations were given the remaining nights for their activities. The village editor of the weekly newspaper was asked to become the clearinghouse for the calendar. When any organization wished a meeting involving the community, the date was cleared by calling the editor. What had been a chaotic situation became orderly. Where conflicts and difficulty had often been apparent, peace ruled. The responsibility for the construction of the community calendar lay in the hands of the young mothers' club. A recent innovation that they have sponsored is sending a calendar to the homes of all the people in the community. Notices of regular meeting nights are printed in spaces under the days of the week throughout the calendar. Enough space was supplied under each day so that each family could write in its additional appointments.

Situation 4. The local church felt the need for family devotions in every home. This was a program that needed the support of every member and organization of the church. Letters were sent from the officers of each organization to each member of that organization emphasizing the need for home devotions. The pastor spoke about this need from the pulpit. In the church school boys and girls of every age level, from the youngest to the oldest, were taught the art of praying. The youngest were taught table, night-time, and morning prayers. The older members of the church school were given instructions in voluntary praying. The youth organization made a study of a section of the Scriptures with special emphasis on its devotional aids. During a special home visitation program, a pamphlet on family devotions was left on the table of every home, along with the devotional material sponsored by the denomination.

The pastor, who recognized that a program of home devotions is most easily instituted directly after a couple are married, started an innovation. After he had married a couple and they had returned from their wedding trip to establish their home, he immediately visited them. He talked to them about the importance of establishing their home, and before he left he took the devotional material of their denomination and conducted a devotional service for the young couple. Then he placed the devotional material in the hands of the husband and authorized him as the high priest in that home to be responsible from that time on for the conducting of family worship.

Situation 5. The local church recognizes that for the best understanding of the Christian evangel it is essential for all its members to know not only the program and outreach of the local church but also the denominational and world outreach of the Christian Church. Part of the over-all program of the church is its missionary outreach. In order to understand and appreciate this phase of the work of the church, one church felt it necessary to instruct all its people at the same time. In order to do this, various groups within the church were made responsible for certain phases of the program. Men furnished the instructional leadership. The women took care of the potluck meals that had to be served. For four Sunday nights all members of the congregation from young to old were invited to attend a "School of Missions." The people sat down to a communal meal. The pastor, as head of the church family, led them in a family type of worship. After the meal, the people separated into age groups and attended classes of instruction that were especially aimed at their age level. The material used in the classes was provided by the denomination and covered the missionary outreach of that denomination. After the program of separate instruction had been completed, the families in units assembled and saw a moving picture covering the mission stations they had studied. Thus, for four consecutive weeks, the educational program was carried on. The result of such a major effort was not hard to see. The interest in missionary outreach was greatly strengthened. The interpretation of personal stewardship was much more vivid on the family level. Thus, again, a local church knowing the needs of its people chose this opportunity to interest its membership both in education and in service.

The situations that have been described were actual ones experienced in rural churches with which the author is familiar. This sort of program is of the highest type. Of course, it is to be recognized that programing of this caliber is possible only through excellent leadership. Pastors in most churches today are capably trained men. With but little imagination and a lot of hard work such plans can be made for almost any church. Again we need to point out that the program as instituted in one church may not function in another. Adaptation to local needs is always paramount.

In the process of building and applying the local program, certain simple factors should always be remembered: (1) What is the need? (2) Does the suggested program fit this need? (3) Are all persons possible being contacted? (4) Has the responsibility for the program been placed upon the largest number of people? (5) Does everyone have an intentionally planned part in some phase of the church's program?

Many times the programs carried out by local churches are mere busywork because the needs of the community and the local people have not been taken into consideration. Mere busywork has no place on the church's calendar.

How Can the Results Be Checked?

Check sheets have been referred to several times in the material of this book. These are obtainable from the denominational headquarters of most churches. Check sheets usually deal in numbers and material growth. It cannot be denied that material growth is a very important factor in the life of the local church. Such growth cannot be ignored. There is always the danger, however, that the measure of a pastor's success may be judged by the material progress which the local church makes. In these days annual reports seem almost entirely dependent upon numbers. (1) So many members were received by transfer, by confession, by reaffirmation. So many members were lost by transfer, by death, by discipline. The net gain or loss was so many. (2) Church school enrollment was increased by ——, for a net gain of ——. The women raised $2,246.61. They have in their treasury $841. (3) The young people raised $541 and have $125 cash on hand. (4) The congregation met all its financial responsibilities and had $2,341 on hand, which was transferred to the building fund.

This is the type of report that a church often makes at its annual meeting. The basis of its effectiveness and its ministry is judged from these figures. It is true that where a strong spiritual program is carried on, the material side usually develops and also becomes strong. However, it is an indication of weakness to base all progress of a church on this structure. It is more important that the following questions be answered in the affirmative, indicating the growth and development of the congregation:

Simple Church Check Sheet

1. Has the spiritual understanding of the people increased?
2. Have the people taken a firmer hold on the essential programing of the Christian church than they had before?
3. Has the understanding of doctrinal and Scriptural truth been increased in the minds of the people?
4. Has this church always maintained an atmosphere conducive to worship?
5. Has this church kept the avenues of service open to all its members?
6. Has this church helped its members to find these avenues of service?
7. Has the ministry to the sick, the bereaved, and the troubled been carried on adequately?
8. Is the physical appearance of the church property a credit to the community?
9. Has the missionary outreach of this church been adequate?

10. Are there evidences that the ministration of the church to the community has lifted the moral and ethical code to a higher level?
11. Is this church active in the lives of its people seven days of the week? (This does not mean that complete activities affecting all the people must be conducted every day in the church.)
12. Has this church recognized its responsibility to the people who have been unreached by any church in this community?
13. Has this church's influence been one of unification in its area or one of fragmentation?

This suggested check sheet deals with general results and is, of course, dependent upon subjective judgment. However, it becomes very essential for the local congregation to answer these more general questions. The second type of check sheet which the local congregation can develop must be based upon the goals which it sets up at the beginning of the time period. Some of these goals might read as follows:

1. Has the pastor visited in every home each year?
2. Is the increase in church school enrollment equal to the increase in population of that age group plus a proportion of boys and girls who have been unreached? (The planning committee may arbitrarily indicate a number: for example, if the public school population has increased by three per cent, then the church school enrollment should increase by three per cent. Add to that the need to cover all unreached children; thus a goal of six per cent increase might appear feasible.)
3. Has the net membership of the church kept in line with the increase of population?
4. Have the proposed property improvements been made?
5. Has the new program of worship through music been successful?
6. Have the significant rural days been observed, such as Harvest Festival, Rogation Sunday?

A check sheet based on the goals that were set up by the church planning committee can be made an invaluable instrument by which the progress toward the achievement of the goals can best be measured. If a large list of these is set up, it might be wise to meet two or three times a year to check progress. If goals have been set up that the check list indicates have not been achieved, these questions should always be asked: (1) Why did the program fail? (2) Who or what was responsible for its failure? (3) Is this goal still desirable? (4) What can be done so that this goal can be achieved?

Many times the failure of a program may be caused by lack of good leadership, the failure to check on progress, or incorrect planning in the first place.

New goals and programing to implement their achievement should be set up only after a careful analysis of the successes and failures of the year before. Failures do not necessarily represent poor leadership or bad planning. They sometimes represent planning for a need that does not exist. Over a period of years the committee that sets up the total program of the church will gain much wisdom and help from the check sheet.

One of the most significant benefits that result from the type of programing suggested in this chapter is the lengthening of a pastor's stay in the local church. Without adequate planning many pastors remain for a very short period of years. Their best work is never accomplished because they do not stay long enough to comprehend the needs of the church and to give to the people their very best planned efforts. By following the suggestion made above, the pastor is challenged to stay long enough so that results may be obtained from long-range planning. A congregation is always anxious to keep a pastor who knows not only how to set up a program but also how to carry it through and check its results.

Careful planning usually results in an awareness that the church has not reached many people living within its community area. This new awareness can stir the congregation to definite action in contacting these people.

Part Three

EXTENDING THE PROGRAM

Chapter 8

THE UNREACHED

THE PERENNIAL PROBLEM of the Christian Church of all ages has been the evangelization of the unreached. One of the major portions of the total program of the Church has centered itself in the solution of this problem. Missionaries have been sent out by the Church both into adjacent areas and into countries beyond the border of the homeland. The work of the Church in America has been no different. When first discoverers and explorers came to this country, the Indians immediately became the center of attention. It has been related that Christopher Columbus baptized hundreds of these natives in mass ceremonies. Almost every section of the United States had its early missionary effort directed toward the Indians, but with the arrival of thousands of immigrants the direction of missionary effort was changed somewhat and aimed not only at the Indians but also at the newly arrived immigrants. A superficial study of our early history would indicate that most of the colonists were strong churchmen. It would seem that from the very start the Christian Church was a major factor in the development of the land. However, this assumption has not been borne out by actual facts. In 1850 only 16 per cent of the population of the country were church members. By 1900 this had risen to 36 per cent. There was a gradual rise from 1900 to 1940, so that by 1940, 49 per cent of our total population belonged to some church. From 1940 to 1953 there was a very precipitous rise in church membership. About 59 per cent of the population are now affiliated with some church.

At the present time the population of the United States is over 160,000,000. Today there remain more than 72,500,000 people in the United States who are members of no church. It can thus readily be seen that in the United States there are large numbers of people to whom the Church needs to hold out its hand in missionary outreach.

Many studies have been made to find out just where these unreached people are to be found. Is it in the large city, the county seat town, the village, or the open country? It is not accurate to say that they may be found in any one of these areas more than in any other. However, indications based on the most accurate studies seem to point to the rural areas.

In the Pacific Northwest, as careful studies seem to show, the largest number of unchurched people are to be found in villages and open country. This may be accounted for in several ways. There is a concentration of churches in most urban areas. In order that these churches may grow, a keen spirit of competition for unreached people in the cities was developed. Population also tended to concentrate in urban areas. This was especially true prior to and during the Second World War. Churches did a good job of contacting and holding people who moved into the urban areas.

On the other hand the churches in the village and country had not gotten a strong hold upon the people. This can be accounted for best by the fact that denominations were interested in following the larger masses of migration rather than the more scattered residents in the villages and open country. Pastors also were more inclined to gravitate toward urban centers, abandoning the rural areas. The leadership in the village and country church was poor and given to extreme conservatism. Consequently large sections of the rural population were untouched. Because of wheat farming and lumbering, the population was scattered, making it more difficult to conduct church work economically. Studies that were made in this section indicated that as much as 74 per cent of the rural population were unchurched.

In the Middle West the picture, though not so extreme, tends to follow the same pattern. Again it must be said that the superficial student of rural life in the Middle West would be likely to state that the rural people are better churched than the urban people. Because of their many opportunities to attend church and affiliate themselves, most rural people belong to some church organization. This again is not a fact. Many studies have been made by students of rural life such as Dr. J. H. Kolb and Edmund de S. Brunner, Dr. W. H. Stacy, Dr. Lowry Nelson, and others. From these studies a sort of Middle Western pattern can be traced. Economically depressed rural areas have a higher percentage of unchurched members than better economic areas. People living in the cities are more likely to be affiliated with the church than those in the country.

The Iowa Christian Rural Fellowship from 1946 to 1948 sponsored religious preference surveys among over 500,000 people in the State of Iowa. These studies showed that slightly more than 12 per cent of the rural people are not affiliated with any church, according to their own statement. These studies also indicated that many of the people who claimed membership in a church were completely inactive so far as participation was concerned. Actually less than 64 per cent of those claiming church membership were active in participating.

Frequently it was noted in these studies that the claim for membership in a local church by individuals was not confirmed by the statistical record of the church concerned. Many people would claim membership in a church when actually that membership was based on their childhood in the church's Sunday school. The picture was strikingly different in urban areas. In one Midwestern city of 40,000, between 70 per cent and 80 per cent of the adult population claimed church membership. In the fringe area of the same city, including two rural townships, the adults who claimed membership numbered less than 36 per cent.

A survey completed in 1952 covering two small cities and an entire county in Wisconsin has pointed out an interesting trend. The more flourishing churches were located in the two small cities. Their outreach and contact with people within the city limits was highly commendable. In fact, in the one city of 5,000 population less than 8 per cent of the total adult population were without a church. The rural area of the same county in which these two cities were located showed quite a different picture. Almost one third of the adult population had no church membership.

The reason for this difference may be attributed to certain factors: (1) The churches in the urban areas were able to command excellent leadership. (2) They had sufficient finances to carry on a well-developed program. (3) They were located in population centers large enough so that the churches could develop into strong institutions. (4) The population was conveniently concentrated so that a large proportion of the pastor's time did not need to be spent on distant calling. (5) The conveniences and cultural advantages of the urban centers helped to hold pastors in the area for a longer period of time than was possible for churches located in rural sections.

On the other hand in the rural areas there were certain factors which worked against a consistently strong church program: (1) The people were scattered. (2) The rural churches located in small villages and open country were too small to be economically sound. (3) Most of the rural churches were able to command only part-time service from their pastors — frequently two or three churches shared one man. (4) The population of the rural area was dwindling. (5) In the sections adjacent to the small cities, the rural area was neglected by the churches located in the cities. This area did not develop its own churches.

The situation in the eastern part of the United States varies considerably. In some states the unchurched rural population has been estimated at over 75 per cent. In other states it approaches much more nearly the Midwestern percentage. However, in almost all locations, the rural population is more likely to have a higher percentage of unreached people than the urban.

When considered from an objective point of view, it would appear as though the solution to the unreached problem is a fairly simple one. To install a progressive leadership in the local church, to develop an attractive program, and to invite the unreached apparently should result in a satisfactory solution. This, however, is not the case. Today it is much more difficult to persuade the unreached that they should affiliate themselves with the local church than it is to take the Christian Church with its claims into an area where it is relatively unknown. Most of the unreached people in America today have a general knowledge of the work of the Church. Many of them have relatives within the Church. Others have had parents that were members of the Church. Consequently they are well acquainted with the ethical standard of the Christian Church. Usually, they conduct themselves within the influence of this standard. Upon being contacted for the church they will say that they are just as good as the people who attend church and consequently do not feel any particular need for or attraction to the local church. Someone has very pointedly described such people as being "inoculated with Christianity, and consequently immune against it."

Thus far in this chapter we have been discussing the unreached people from the point of view of the church. It has become apparent that the larger percentage of these people live in rural areas and that the responsibility for contacting and winning them rests upon the rural church. There is, however, another side to this picture. To find out why so large a segment of rural population remains unreached by the church, the author contacted a large sampling who, on their own admission, were not church-related. It was not always possible to elicit answers to the questions which he placed. However, a high percentage of the sampling replied to the question, "Why are you not connected with some church?" The answers have been summarized as follows:

1. "The church has never contacted either me or any member of my family." These people felt that the initial step needed to be taken by the church. In the urban area where competition for church affiliation has been comparatively strong, the churches have contacted the unreached again and again. In the rural area this has not been true. Pastors on limited financial budgets have found it impossible to expend the money needed to contact scattered families. Another factor found among rural churchmen has worked against a consistent outreach program. Pastors steeped in a sort of traditional theology have stated categorically to the author that their building is open on Sunday, the gospel is preached. If the unreached are to be contacted, the Holy Spirit will drive them to the church.

2. "The church is too far distant from our home." Many times people who have given this response also indicated on their schedule that a certain town was their shopping center. It was not too far to drive five or six miles to this center. However, if the church was more than three miles from their homes, it was too far distant to attend. When pressed on this point, they explained that they themselves did not attend church, but they would like their children in

Sunday school. However, since the children could not drive the car and the church was too far distant to walk, no church connection was made.

3. "The churches fight too much." This statement usually meant that there were too many churches in a given area and the competition for members had developed into a brawl. The one church criticized the other and frequently went so far as to claim that only those who belonged to this one particular denomination would have hope for "eternal salvation." All others were outside of the chosen group. The unreached who gave this reason indicated that they therefore preferred not to affiliate with any church.

4. "The church is all right, but I am too busy with my work." This excuse was particularly evident in dairying sections of the country. Where large herds of cattle were being milked and much feeding was carried on, people found it difficult on Sundays to attend church. Thus, rather than be limited in their attendance, they chose not to be affiliated with the church.

5. "The church is O.K. but I have never thought about joining it." A large number of people in this sampling in their answers indicated an ignorance about the purpose of the church and as a consequence were entirely indifferent to its program. They had never gotten acquainted with its work and consequently could not be expected to show any interest.

Many other reasons were given, some of which were quite legitimate. Lack of adequate leadership in the church, a part-time ministry, no regular services, and a poorly planned program were additional reasons set forth by the people of this sampling.

It was not possible to place in any particular category the people who remained unreached by the church. It wasn't particularly the newcomer in the community, nor the couple with a large family, nor the economic underprivileged, nor the socially unadjusted. They seemed to come from almost every classification. There were those who no longer had children at home, who were retired or on the verge of retirement, and who had slipped away from the church. There were those who held responsible community positions, or were operators of well-organized farm enterprises. There were those who were somewhat economically depressed and had large families.

Among all the excuses and explanations of the high percentage of unreached people in rural areas as given by both the church and the people affected, the most common on both sides need to be given serious consideration. They deal with poor leadership, inadequate programing, and a haphazard approach. That so high a proportion of unreached people are to be found in the rural areas of our land is a major challenge to the leadership within the town and country churches.

Many of the leaders in these churches have never recognized this need or challenge. A good example of this came to light not very long ago. A young man was called to his first pastorate out of seminary. He chose the rural field because he felt in it was to be found the largest opportunity for outreach. After he had gotten acquainted with the people in his church, he had a meeting with his official board and suggested to the members that a careful house-to-house survey be made within five miles of the church to discover any unreached families. Members of the board smiled indulgently at their young pastor and informed him that there were no unreached families in the area. These members of the board had lived in the surrounding territory most of their lives. They knew all the people personally. The young pastor accepted the word of his board members. However, after two years had passed, he began to realize there were some people in the surrounding area with whom he had gotten acquainted through business contacts who did not seem to have church relationships. He succeeded in persuading his young people to make a house-to-house canvass within a five-mile circle of his church. After the study had been made, he had the names of forty-four families who claimed no church relationship. At the next meeting of his official board he announced the result of the survey. The board members immediately inquired the names of these unreached families. As the young pastor mentioned a name, a trustee would say, "Oh, but I know that his father always attended our church." When another name was mentioned, a deacon spoke up and said, "Why, his grandmother belonged to the Bethel Lutheran Church."

To solve the problem of outreach is one of the major challenges of the town and country church. Some of the techniques of the past are still valuable today, but new tools have been developed. Some of the most effective ones need to be described.

Methods of Outreach

As stated above one of the major problems facing the rural church is to win those who are outside of its membership. If these can be added to the membership of the town and country churches, many attendant problems will be solved. Finances will be more adequate, better leadership will be obtained, and a broader program can be planned.

There are no techniques or lines of action that will invariably fit every need. However, there are some that have proved very worthwhile.

In Chapter 5 an explanation was made of how to conduct a house-to-house religious survey. This survey is one of the absolutely essential steps that must be taken before developing techniques of outreach. Assuming that this has been done and that a careful analysis of information has been compiled, the local church will next develop a program of planned calling. This has been referred to both in this book and elsewhere as lay evangelism. It is not sufficient merely to set up teams of two each to be assigned to certain areas for the purpose of contacting the unreached. These teams need to be briefed very carefully in the methods of correct approach. A school of instruction should be set up and taught by the pastor or someone else who is familiar with the best methods of lay evangelism. It is not merely essential to press the claims of the local church on the individual. The teams should be familiar with the deeper purposes of evangelistic calling. They should be able to press the claims of Jesus Christ on each person, emphasizing that person's relationship to the Christian religion rather than his relationship to the local church. This does not mean that the latter should not be done. Rather, it means that the former is primary and the latter naturally develops out of it. Usually this kind of evangelism centers around certain periods of the year. Lent and Easter have always played an important part in lay visitation. Rally Day in the fall and Christmas time have also been used.

Certain dangers are to be recognized in a program of lay evangelism. The high spirit of enthusiasm gradually dies out if no consistent follow-up program is devised. Another weakness in the program is the fact that after a period of lay visitation no continued plan is carried through. People who are outside of the church need repeated and constant attention if they are eventually to become affiliated with it.

The follow-up activity after a period of lay visitation depends largely upon the pastor. The results accomplished by the various teams are turned over to him. He then needs to call on every good prospect who has been discovered by the visitation teams. Frequently this additional touch will swing the balance in favor of the church.

Another method of outreach is through a consistent program of church publicity. Where this has been used, it has been found especially effective. After the house-to-house survey has been completed and the local church has determined its natural community (see Chapter 2), a mailing list carefully composed of those who are affiliated with the church and those whom the church wishes to contact who have no religious relationships should be developed. News about the activity of the church, selected articles concerning its organizations, information about the national and international outreach of the church, and other related materials can carefully be mimeographed and sent out as a monthly church paper. Pastoral letters that deal with the family and its religious welfare should also be sent out at regular intervals. As this material comes into the homes at regular times over a period of years, the doors are frequently opened to make it possible to win the unchurched families. Just as the constant dripping of water will wear away rock, so the constant appearance of information from the church will wear away the resistance that some families have toward it.

In line with this publicity, special invitations should be sent out to the children of unreached families. These invitations may cover such events as the Sunday school picnic, Christmas celebration, Rally Day, and the vacation church school. Thus the attention of the children will also be focused on the activities of the church.

Newspaper publicity, although it has its place in the life of the church, is not likely to have much effect upon people who are outside the organization; therefore, it cannot be depended upon as a major vehicle of evangelization.

A third line of action that a church may take centers itself in the public school. Many school systems in various states permit the local pastors, if they work co-operatively, to take a religious census of the students in the school. Children are given cards to take home and fill out with the aid of their parents. These cards will indicate church relationship or the lack of such among the students. Usually after such an approach, a program of Christian education based on released time from school activities is set up. This technique can best be used where schools center themselves through consolidation in the village or town in which the churches present a united program to the school authorities. In many cases children from nonchurch-related homes attend the released-time classes and thus eventually are won to allegiance in a local church.

A most effective program of outreach is the platoon system. The author has personally used this system and has directed students in their externship year in its use. If very carefully organized and supervised, this system can be more effective than any thus far discussed.

The platoon system is developed as follows: The community in which the local church operates and which it plans to cover is carefully divided into geographical sections. In the country these divisions may be four square miles or less, depending upon the density of population. In the villages they may be a block, certain streets, or a combination of these. A member of the church living within a division, or adjacent to it, is appointed as the person responsible for this particular area. Because the membership is not always strategically located to cover a complete community area, it may be necessary to start out with only a segment of the community in this plan. After appointments have been made, all those who have been assigned territory are called together for a meeting in order to receive their instructions. The following items of importance are placed under their jurisdiction: (1) Each one is to report to the pastor all families in his territory that are not actively connected with any church. (2) When a new renter takes over a farm or a home, his name and address are to be reported to the pastor. (3) Any illness among those related to the local church or among families that are not related to any church should immediately be reported to the pastor. (4) Whenever land or a home is sold, the purchaser's name and address should be reported. (5) Any other need that becomes evident, if it relates itself to the church, should also be noted.

Here is a typical example of how this system works, taken from an actual experience. George Knox, an absentee landowner, sold his farm to a young couple who lived two hundred miles distant but planned to move to the farm the following March 1. The George Jansen family was responsible for this area. Immediately George notified the pastor that this farm had changed hands and that the young couple, Mr. and Mrs. James Sands, who had purchased it, lived at Red Leaf, Minnesota. The pastor sat down at his typewriter and wrote Mr. and Mrs. Sands a letter, telling them about the community and especially about the church and its activities. He indicated that he was happy that they were coming into the community and that he hoped they would find an adequate place of service in the area. The Sands family were put on the mailing list of the church, and the monthly church paper, the pastoral letters, and the church bulletins were sent to them during the months of November through February. Early in February the pastor wrote another personal letter asking them to let him know the date of their arrival with their household goods and their truckloads of cattle and machinery. The pastor stated in his letter that a crew of men would be present to help them to unload and get settled in their new home. A letter was received from the Sandses telling of their arrival by midafternoon, March 1. The pastor contacted George Jansen and asked him to line up a crew of men to help to get the young couple settled. Everything went according to schedule. The cattle were bedded down in short order. The furniture was placed in the house. Mrs. Jansen asked the young couple to come over for supper that night. After they had eaten and were ready to go back to their new home, George invited them to the services at the church on Sunday. He stated that he and Mrs. Jansen and their children would pick them up in time for Sunday school and introduce them to members of the congregation. When Sunday arrived, there was no question about church attendance. The Sandses were brought to the church by the Jansens and in a very short time were integrated into the ongoing life of that local church. This example can be multiplied by many similar ones.

It is very important that the people who have been made responsible for a given area shall have an opportunity to meet to discuss their experiences. Consequently, once every four months the pastor should call his " lieutenants " together for a discussion meeting. He should point out how this system has worked and how helpful it has been to him. Some method should be devised by which this responsibility can be passed around to other families. As the church develops, additional segments of the community should be covered. Over a period of ten years this carefully organized program will do much toward winning the unreached to the local church.

There are many other methods that have been used successfully by churches in the contact of the unreached. The method, though important, is not the deciding factor. The regularity, constant alertness, and sincerity of the church's leadership are more significant. If genuine concern is felt for the unreached, success in contacting them will be much more apparent.

Chapter 9

THE DENOMINATIONAL PARISH

As has been stated in Chapter 1, there are certain economic and population factors that make it improbable that all the local churches in a given town and country area will become strong, self-supporting organizations. Dwindling population in rural areas and an overabundance of local churches make it very difficult to carry on all phases of a well-rounded church program. Sometimes entire departments in the Sunday church school are missing. The youth organizations of high school age are so depleted in numbers that the few young people who attend become disinterested. More than a quarter of a century ago, church leaders devised a plan whereby the approach of church work to a given community was made co-operatively by a number of churches rather than by one single organization. This plan became well known as the larger parish plan. Theoretically all the churches in a given area, irrespective of denomination, were asked to work together in this program. Many difficulties arose, and in frequent instances the program failed. More of this will be discussed in the following chapter. In recent years a variation of the larger parish has been developed on the denominational level. This plan has resulted in more success than the original larger parish. In order to differentiate it from the interdenominational larger parish, we shall call it the denominational co-operative parish program.

Frequently in town and country areas within the limits of twenty-five to forty miles, a number of churches adhering to one denomination have developed. When our immigrant forefathers came into this country, they sometimes took over as an ethnic group a segment of territory equivalent to a county. Because they had similar backgrounds and were from the same ethnic origins, one denomination prevailed in the area. Sometimes there were eight or nine Lutheran churches or Methodist churches or Presbyterian churches, all within easy driving range. This does not mean that there were no churches of other denominations in the area. Usually, many other churches were also to be found. Because of many factors, already touched on in this book, the churches of this predominant denomination did not become strong and large economic units. Many carried on a woefully inadequate program. Church leaders realized that the first level of co-operation could develop most easily on the denominational basis. Only as churches of the same denomination in an adjacent area are willing to work together, dare one expect co-operation on the interdenominational level. Consequently where churches of one denomination are thus strategically located, the co-operative parish is the answer to many of the rural church problems.

The Denominational Co-operative Parish Defined and Explained

A co-operative parish consists of three or more churches belonging to the same denomination located in a larger rural community working together as though they were one congregation with similar purposes to serve all the people of that denomination and those others unreached in the area with a carefully organized and complete program administered by a diversified ministry.

The first step in the development of a co-operative parish begins on the level of the church leadership within the larger rural area. Pastors and lay leaders who are concerned about the inadequacy of their local church and its inefficiency in programing come together for a period of discussion. Generally, this first gathering of leadership is suggested or directed by outside denominational leadership that has grown concerned about certain local situations. Of course, it is much better if the initial steps are taken by the local people themselves.

At this first gathering the needs of the local churches concerned are discussed. Their weakness and strength are brought into focus with each other. Frequently some of these churches are supplied by only a partial ministry. They share their pastor's time with some other church, but actually there is no other relationship between the churches thus sharing their pastoral leadership. At this first meeting examples of co-operative parishes are studied. The leadership itself must become convinced that in this parish program lies the solution for many of their own local problems.

After the leadership within the churches has become convinced, the next step is that of educating the local congregation. It is in this step that too frequently an inadequate job is done. The churches do not thoroughly understand what is involved. In fact, in some cases no program of local education is carried out. The ineffectiveness of some co-operative parishes today stems from the fact that this second step was either omitted or done inadequately.

The lay and pastoral leaders who have become convinced of the value of the co-operative parish need to explain it to the official church board and also to members of the congregation. This should be done in two ways. First, by way of pastoral letters sent directly into the homes of the people. Descriptions of functioning parishes should be sent to the members of the congregations for publicity purposes. After this has been done, a congregational meeting follows. At this meeting either the pastor with his lay leader or someone well versed in the way of co-operative parishes should again explain the functioning of a parish and the reasons that the local congregation should participate in one. Sample constitutions should be placed in the hands of the people. A long period of discussion should then follow so that all questions may be adequately answered. Objections should be fairly met. It is never wise to withhold any information from the people in the local churches.

The third step is the vote of confidence on the part of the local congregation and the appointment of a committee to carry on negotiations with the other churches involved for the purpose of developing a co-operative parish. This committee may be composed of five members from each local church: (1) the pastor, (2) a member of the official board, (3) a representative from the women's organization, (4) a member at large, and (5) a member from the youth group.

The committees from the various churches involved will then meet, giving at least a half day's time to the preliminary organization of the co-operative parish. A temporary constitution should be set up. In this preliminary constitution will appear the description of the activities of the parish, its official organization, the relationship of each church to the parish, and a definition of duties and obligations.

This document should then be returned to each congregation for approval and the congregation should vote itself into the parish as a member.

Suggestions Toward the Development of a Constitution for a Co-operative Parish

The following suggestions have been developed by Alfred Behrer, Co-ordinator of the Rock River Co-operative Parish, Taylor Ridge, Illinois, and the author.

Name

The name of the parish shall be the Ideal Co-operative Parish.

Purpose

1. To promote co-operation between the individual churches and their members.
2. To help one another in the social, educational, and religious work of the parish through co-operation with one another.
3. To sponsor and develop activities in the parish that will widen and deepen the faith of the membership in God and the work of the Church both at home and abroad.
4. To provide sufficient financial support for a parish program.
5. To provide adequate leadership for all the people within the bounds of the parish.
6. To make possible a full program for every church.

Bounds of Parish Constituents

1. Any church within the parish bounds may become a member by a two-thirds vote of any regularly called congregational meeting, by its willingness to participate in the projects of the parish, by accepting the constitution, and by electing members to the parish council. This action is subject to the approval of presbytery, district, classis, conference, etc.
2. The church which becomes a member shall maintain its prerogatives as a church. It selects its own minister, it retains its system of government, it controls its own financial policy and disbursements of all monies.

3. Any church may withdraw if the council has been given a written notice of its intention two months in advance and by a two-thirds congregational vote.
4. All persons who are members of the co-operating churches shall also be members of the co-operative parish.

The Parish Council

1. The parish council shall be the governing body of the co-operative parish.
2. The parish council shall be composed of five representatives from each participating church:
   a. The minister.
   b. One from the session, official board, or corresponding body.
   c. A member from the women's organizations.
   d. A representative of the young people.
   e. A member at large.
3. The council members shall be elected at the annual meeting of the congregation and shall serve for a period of three years with the exception of the minister, who will be a permanent member of the council.
4. A rotary system shall be set up, and for the beginning year one shall be elected for one year, one for two years, and two for three years. After the first year, each representative will be elected to serve for three years. No member can succeed himself in office, but he can be re-elected after an intervening period of one year.
5. The council shall plan the program and activities of the parish.

Officers

1. The officers of the council shall be:
   a. Co-ordinator.
   b. Associate co-ordinator.
   c. Secretary.
   d. Treasurer.

   No officer shall succeed himself for more than one term without an intervening year, with the exception of the co-ordinator.
2. The co-ordinator shall be an ordained minister of one of the co-operating churches and in good and regular standing of his denomination. He will be elected by the council for a period of three

years, subject to the approval of the local governing body of the denomination (presbytery, district, conference, classis, etc.). His duties shall be:

   a. To preside at all meetings of the council except as he requests the associate co-ordinator to do so.
   b. To be an ex officio member of all committees.
   c. To lead the council, committees, and parish in all projects undertaken.
   d. To execute the program that has been planned by the council.

3. The associate co-ordinator shall preside in the absence of the co-ordinator or upon his request and shall perform other duties delegated to him. He shall be elected for three years.
4. The secretary shall keep an accurate record of all proceedings of the council (both recording and financial) and shall notify all members at least ten days before the meeting of the council and shall notify all the committees of the duties delegated to them by the council. He shall be elected for one year.
5. The treasurer shall keep all the monies of the council and shall pay out only when directed to do so by the council. He shall make a financial report at each meeting. He shall submit the treasurer's books for audit annually. He shall be elected for one year.

Duties of the Parish Council

1. To plan the over-all program for all churches concerned and to implement the enactment of the program.
2. To assign parish responsibilities.
3. To plan the extension of the parish program to areas within the parish not reached by any church.
4. To develop publicity through a parish paper.
5. To plan a parish budget and develop means of raising money for the budget.
6. To explain to and assist member churches in the enactment of denominational programs.
7. To be responsible for adequate services to all member churches.
8. To take action in all areas of church work within the parish that can best be developed by the organization as a unit.

Meetings

1. The council will meet quarterly in January, April, July, and October on the second Monday evening of the designated month.
2. At each meeting the council will decide the hour and place of the following meeting.
3. Each meeting shall be opened and closed with prayer.
4. Provision shall be made for special meetings of the council called by the co-ordinator, or, in his inability to do so, by the secretary or by the request of five members of the council, four of whom must be from different churches. The secretary shall notify the members at least ten days in advance of such meetings. Any necessary business relating to the work of the council may be carried on at this meeting.
5. There shall be at least two public meetings per year for the whole parish.
6. A simple majority of the council members will constitute a quorum.

Committees

1. *Executive Committee* of the council shall be composed of the officers of the council and the chairmen of the various committees. This group shall have the power for emergency business subject to the approval of the council at its next regular meeting.
2. *Committee on Youth Work:* This committee will be responsible for all the youth work carried on in the parish and will aid the individual church in its youth program when asked to do so.
3. *Music Committee:* This committee shall act to further the musical interest and participation of the churches in the parish, and shall plan together with the director of music in the event one is employed.
4. *Committee on Adult Work:* This committee will have the responsibility of the men's and women's work in the parish and in aiding individual churches when asked.
5. *Committee on Leadership Training:* This committee will be responsible for setting up leadership training schools, and shall sponsor additional leadership programs.
6. *Publicity Committee* will be responsible for the publication of a

parish newspaper and other publicity essential to the work of the parish.

7. Other committees may be set up by the council as the need arises.

Finances

1. The program will be financed by contributions or assessments from each of the member churches and other denominational agencies. All funds will be paid into the parish treasury.
2. The treasurer shall pay all bills only upon order of the council.

Amendment

This constitution may be amended by a two-thirds vote of the parish council provided that the amendment has been submitted in writing at the previous meeting of the council (that is, the meeting before the vote is to be taken).

Bylaws

Bylaws may be added as the council feels need for additional direction. For passage of proposed bylaws a simple majority vote of the council is required.

Explanations Covering the Proposed Constitution

1. The success or failure of a co-operative parish depends upon a careful statement of purposes for its organization and development. These purposes should not be worded in indefinite or general terms, but should distinctly identify and clarify each reason and purpose for the development of a co-operative parish. It is not necessary to indicate the technique and method by which the purpose will be accomplished. That can be worked out later by the parish council. These purposes are usually based upon two major factors: (*a*) The inadequacy of the local church program, its weakness and its lack of leadership. (*b*) The second major factor is from the positive point of view. Some of the churches within the parish will have certain strong points and will be able to make a major contribution to the strengthening of the less fortunate churches. For example, in one parish there was a church that had developed an excellent choir. Its leadership was good, its music very acceptable, and its appearance excellent. Other churches within this parish were not so fortunate.

The first church went throughout the parish with its choir, practicing with the choirs of the other churches and singing on the Sabbath in conjunction with the choir of the church it visited. Over a period of time this helped the other local choirs to improve considerably.

2. The constituent churches within the parish should be within convenient driving range. It is also quite important that the people of these churches have many things in common. They should be within a natural or geographical area. Because this deals with a denominational parish, the churches should all be affiliated with the same body.

It is very important to point out that none of the usual prerogatives of the local church need to be surrendered to the parish. Each church should have the right to select its own leadership; each church should retain its own system of government and should control its own financial policy. It is also to be noted that constituent churches by a two-thirds congregational vote retain the right to withdraw from the parish.

3. The governing body of the parish is the parish council, which is made up of representatives, usually four or five, from each local church. This council should meet at least four times a year. Three major activities are carried on at these council meetings.

a. The actual development of a program is the first major responsibility of the council.
b. The education of council members in the ongoing program of the denomination is a second function. Council members then become the responsible agents to bring the denominational program home to the local church.
c. The council needs also to review the accomplishments of the parish from quarter to quarter and from year to year, for the purpose of determining the successes and failures and of building upon past relationships and activities.

4. The number of officers and their responsibilities can be determined when the constitution is developed. However, a co-ordinator or parish director must always be one of the officers. Usually, he is one of the pastors of the constituent churches. He may be especially appointed by action of the ecclesiastical body controlling the local churches. His responsibility is usually divided between the parish

and one of the churches. He must see to it that the program set up by the council is implemented into action and that the over-all plans of the parish are co-ordinated into definite action. Actually, the parish council holds him responsible for the enactment of the program.

Because of the high responsibility placed upon the shoulders of the co-ordinator, he should have training in this specialized field of service. A number of seminaries are at the present time giving courses in church administration specifically aimed at the development of able parish co-ordinators. Some seminaries as well as denominations conduct short courses for this purpose. It is not easy for a pastor without this specialized training to take over a parish co-ordinatorship successfully.

5. The parish council, in order to facilitate programing, appoints committees whose responsibility is in one specific area. For example, a committee may be responsible for youth work, another for adult work, a third for leadership training, a fourth for publicity, a fifth for vacation church school work, etc. These committees need to meet before the council does to map out their particular segment of the over-all program. They will then submit their planning to the parish council. This method of specific assignment will facilitate the planning and programing within the parish.

6. The financing of a co-operative parish is one of the most difficult knots to untangle. Experience has proved that more conflict comes from inadequate financing than from any other portion of parish responsibility. The following financial responsibilities are usually a part of the parish:

a. A portion of the co-ordinator's salary, if not the entire salary, must be paid from the parish treasury. The churches keep their own program of finances, pay their own pastor, and take care of their own local expenses as well as benevolent contributions.

b. If a Christian education worker is hired for the entire parish, this money must also be paid from the parish treasury.

c. The traveling expenses of the parish co-ordinator and others who take on parish-wide responsibilities must be met by the central treasury.

d. Since most parishes publish a monthly newssheet and also have other office expenses, these too must be met from the central treasury.

e. Any visual-aid materials and equipment that are used on a parish basis must also be paid for from the parish treasury.

The question arises, How are these expenses to be met? A single solution would be to assess the member churches for their proportionate share. In most cases these churches are marginal ones and, as a consequence, unable to meet this additional burden. This is especially true when the co-operative parish is first developed. As a result, other sources of income must be explored. However, before some are suggested, it is important to state that each church should contribute every year to the support of the parish, even though the sum is not sufficient to meet all expenses. This is a discipline in stewardship that is very important. Experience has shown in mission work that where the monies are allocated from the outside and no responsibility is placed upon the receiving group, a philosophy of financial irresponsibility and selfishness results.

Many times the ecclesiastical body that has supervision over the constituent churches in a parish will contribute a large proportion of the cost of parish operation. These monies are taken from home or national missions funds.

Many of the actual activities of the parish can be financed through the activity itself. For example, youth rallies will usually pay for themselves by registration fees and offerings. The same is true with leadership training schools, men's gatherings, choir festivals, parish picnics, etc.

Another source of income can be made possible through the utilization of the Lord's Portion Plan. If members of the constituent churches who live on the land will allocate a portion of their increase to this purpose, much financial help can result. Harvest festivals, in which these "Lord's portions" are brought together and sold for the benefit of the parish, may be held in two or three strategically located parts of the parish. People who live in villages and towns who wish also to contribute to the parish treasury may do so by giving their services, a day's labor, or, as one hardware merchant did, five per cent of a day's sales.

The actual financing of a parish requires ingenuity. Although it is difficult—as can be seen from the foregoing discussion—it is a challenge that can be met and overcome.

There are certain limiting factors that will determine the possibility of developing a co-operative parish. The first of these, as has been pointed out, depends upon the number of available churches within a given geographical area that adhere to the same denomination. Another limiting factor is the togetherness of the people involved. Where their occupation is similar and their interests are drawn close together, a co-operative parish can exist without major difficulty. Finances will also determine the extent of a parish program. In some cases only token parishes exist because of inadequate finances.

In spite of limiting factors, where the possibility exists to develop a co-operative parish, every reasonable effort should be made to plan one. The results are usually beyond expectation. In many cases churches that had become static in growth took on new life and new members rapidly after the organization of a parish. Sunday schools became more effective. Vacation church schools enrolled two and three times the number of pupils. Many of the buildings and much of the property were improved. Financing for the local church gained in strength. Contributions to national and world missions rose significantly.

Even more important than these outward indications of success was the spirit of understanding that developed among people of churches that were formerly isolated one from the other. A new mutuality and togetherness could be observed. Young people were able to find satisfactions in each other's company that were not possible when the individual church carried on a separate and inadequate program. The social and recreational values were also greatly enhanced. Many other values that remain unmeasurable were also attained through the new parish program.

Chapter 10

THE INTERDENOMINATIONAL PARISH

THE ACTUAL DEVELOPMENT of the interdenominational larger parish preceded the organization of the denominational co-operative parish. Experiences that followed the development of the interdenominational parish pointed the way to the more successful development and operation of the co-operative parish. Although there is much similarity between the two organizations, and although they are set up to perform quite similar tasks, there are also several striking differences that need to be explained and discussed.

The first of these differences is in the relationship of the ministerial leadership within the parish. In the co-operative parish each pastor is usually called by one of the participating churches and is regularly installed as pastor over that church. Then each carries on a specific task in regard to the parish as a whole. One may have oversight in music, another in Christian education, a third in men's work, etc. In the larger parish the pastors called as ministers are not obtained by the local churches, but rather by the larger parish council. This council is responsible for providing the leadership in the constituent churches. Although these ministers may then be assigned to responsibilities in individual churches, they nevertheless are hired by the governing council of the parish. The larger parish director is responsible for the over-all program of the parish as well as for the separate programs of the constituent churches. He directs the entire program and assigns the responsibilities to his staff. The staff relationship to the parish director is to be described somewhat as the relationship of assistant pastors to the directing pastor of a large urban church.

Another difference between these two types of parishes is evident in the responsibilities of the various churches to their separate denominations. In the co-operative parish the same denominational program pertains in every church. The local planning can all be centered around the over-all program of the denomination. This results in a minimum of overlapping and a maximum of efficiency. In the larger interdenominational parish the picture is quite different. There may be churches that have their allegiance to four different denominations, all participating in the parish. The program of these four denominations may be quite different both in emphasis and in procedure. The consequence of this is that the larger parish must develop an independent program outside of the scope of denominational influence. Yet this planning must not be so divergent that it competes with the denominational program. Concessions must be made by both sides. The parish program must frequently give way to denominational programs. On the other hand, the denominational program frequently must limit its scope in favor of the local planning. This same problem is also evident in the acquiring of leadership; whether that leadership shall be in the same proportion as denominations represented or whether that leadership is hired because of the contribution it can make to the local situation is a problem that attends the larger parish.

A third major difference that must be overcome is that of finances. In the co-operative parish it is necessary to deal with but one denomination. In the interdenominational parish it is necessary to deal with a number of denominations. To persuade these to invest funds in the parish is much more difficult than in the former case.

Also, because the parish director and his staff are paid entirely from the larger parish treasury, the churches co-operating in this venture must surrender a large portion of their financing directly to the central treasury. The local expense, such as upkeep of property, janitor services, taxes, heat, and utilities, must be paid out of the separate local treasuries. On the other hand, salaries are paid from the central treasury. This means that the unit churches must surrender some of their financial prerogatives to the central group. It has always been found difficult to persuade constituent churches to take this step. However, where the step has been taken, the results have usually been satisfactory.

A fourth difficulty that has been experienced in the interdenominational parish deals with the program of camping and youth which the constituent denominations carry on. The parish makes every attempt to unify the work of the young people and to develop a desirable program for all of them. Then, during summer camp periods, the various denominations make their bid for their own young people. Thus they separate the youth that have been working together on the parish level. The actual togetherness that the parish program has been attempting to develop is disintegrated by the denominational program.

There are many other minor difficulties that result in an interdenominational larger parish. However, there are so many major beneficial contributions that it is very much worth the effort whenever possible to organize the interdenominational larger parish.

In very recent years a new trend has developed in the interdenominational parish, the organization of which is much looser than under the parish just described. A rather successful example of this newer type has been developed during the past three years in Grant County, Wisconsin. A description of this parish can best explain this newer type of organization.

Grant County, Wisconsin, is located in the southwest corner of the state. It is bordered on the west by the Mississippi River and on the north by the Wisconsin River. A strong one third of its territory is composed of rough farming country. The remainder is composed of fair to good arable land. There are only two small urban centers in the county, one with a population of 3,000 and the other with a population of 5,000. The remainder of the county is made up of little villages and open country farms. The people came from various sources to settle this county. There were German artisans, Welsh miners, Norwegian farmers, and Luxemburger farmers; there was also a sprinkling of New Englanders. During the course of years, after the settling of Grant County, other groups have also made their homes in the area. The people of the county by heritage were predominantly Protestant. The Luxemburgers were Roman Catholic. Many small churches dotted the countryside as well as the villages and towns. Methodist, Primitive Methodist, Evangelical United Brethren, Evangelical and Reformed, Congregational, Presbyterian,

Baptist, and Lutheran predominated.

About five years ago it became evident that the trend in these churches was downward. Many of the smaller units had been closed. Some of the stronger churches were gradually weakening. At a meeting held by denominational executives to discuss their church programs in Wisconsin, their attention was directed to Grant County, and it was determined that a careful study should be made to find out just what had been happening during the past years. This study was made by the author. First a statistical study from the yearbooks of the affected denominations was undertaken. Twenty-five years of Protestantism were closely examined, and charts of progress or of retrogression were made. Immediately it became apparent that all the denominations in the area were declining in influence and in numbers. Even though smaller, poorly financed churches had been closed, the membership of the closed units did not seem to strengthen any of the surrounding congregations. This information and these charts were presented to the denominational executives and to lay church leaders of the county. They all felt that some action should be taken, more information should be gathered, and some kind of interdenominational organization should be set up. They agreed to meet again after this information had been made available.

Pastors of local churches and students from the University of Dubuque made house-to-house spot surveys in most sections of the county. These exact studies definitely pointed out the trends of disintegration for Protestantism. About one third of the population of the entire county gave no church affiliation in these surveys. At another meeting of laymen, pastors, and executives, it was decided to organize a larger parish into a loose organization to be called the Grant County Fellowship of Churches. A proposed constitution was drawn up and the laymen submitted this constitution to their local churches. Thirty churches voted eventually to become participants.

The particular weaknesses of the Protestant Church program in the county became apparent from the studies that had been made. The first order of business for the Fellowship was to get under way the kind of planned program that would overcome these apparent weaknesses and strengthen the entire approach of Protestantism in Grant County.

There was a distinct overchurching in certain areas which resulted in excessive competition and strife between groups. Denominational executives felt that they could make their major contribution at this point. Where local churches could be served by one pastor, such arrangements were made. For example, in two adjacent villages, a United Brethren pastor living in a Methodist parsonage serves both the Methodist and United Brethren churches. Thus, these two churches, which might have been in competition with each other, now work together without losing their relationship to their own denomination. In another section where six struggling Methodist churches had worked quite independently of each other, within the bounds of the Grant County Fellowship they have developed their own co-operative parish, thus again bringing a united front of Protestantism to bear upon that area.

A Fellowship council composed of representative laymen and pastors from each church worked together in the development of a needed program in the entire area. Many of the small churches lacked trained leadership. One of the major contributions made by the Fellowship was the development of two leadership training schools, strategically located in the county so that members of all the participating churches interested in leadership training could with little effort attend the schools. The results have been far beyond expectation both in the numbers that attended and in the value of the instruction.

An annual picnic is held by the Fellowship. This picnic brings all the families of the constituent churches together in a central location. Congregationalists and Presbyterians, Methodists and Evangelical Reformed find common ties in the social friendships established at these picnics.

During the first year of the Fellowship's existence, it was decided to hold daily vacation church schools in every section of the county so far as it was possible to do so. A young woman who was a student in a local teachers college carried the major responsibility. Church schools were held in schools, churches, abandoned store buildings, and farm homes. Children who had never had the opportunity of participating in a vacation school enjoyed their first experience. The number of boys and girls receiving instruction was far beyond that of any former year when vacation church schools were operated independent of and isolated from each other.

In many of these churches few young people of high school and junior high school ages could be reached. In fact, many of the churches had so small a number of young people that a program could not be carried on. Youth rallies were developed on both the sectional and the county level. Thus the young people from every part of the county had fellowship with other church-minded young people.

As is often the case in small churches, the problem of music was very acute. In Grant County at the very start of the program it was determined that something needed to be done in this field. A choir festival was organized. Certain selections of choir music were made and sent to each individual church. People interested in singing were taught these pieces and became familiar with the music score. Then they were brought together at a central location, and a trained musician directed them in a day's practice. On the following Sabbath afternoon they were again brought together to present a festival of music. The author attended one of these at which over 250 people participated in the choir and sang before an appreciative audience of more than one thousand.

It would not be fair to give the impression that the development of the Fellowship has always been marked with success. There have also been failures. A program for the development and appreciation of rural life was set up by a committee. National leadership was obtained. Invitations were sent out, not only to the families of the constituent churches, but to the 41,000 inhabitants of the entire county. Arrangements were made to meet at the Teachers College in Platteville. The day dawned warm and beautiful. Less than sixty people attended the conference. Most of those attending were in some capacity of leadership in the Fellowship. Other failures in the area of men's work might also be cited. However, the over-all results have been more gratifying and in certain areas phenomenal.

As has been indicated, certain concessions by the denominations must be made when this type of larger parish is attempted. For example, at least four of the major denominations represented hold semiannual youth rallies. The Fellowship rallies would be likely to interfere with the success of the denominational ones. As a consequence denominational rallies are not held. However, when the Fellowship holds a rally, forty-five minutes of the time is given to each denomination to gather its own young people so that the ongoing program of the denomination may be explained to them.

Recently, a much more thoroughgoing religious-preference survey has been completed. Some very interesting factors have come to light. One of the major ones is that farm young people are not being contacted by the churches which are usually situated at the marketing centers. The 4-H clubs are doing a much more efficient job in youth contact and conservation than are the churches.

Other factors also became quite apparent. As a result of this study the members of the council of the Fellowship have determined to take several steps.

They proposed to set up a program of evangelistic outreach that will contact all the unreached in the county. They hope to develop a plan by which teams, irrespective of denomination, will work together.

They plan a more extensive program in Christian education. This will center itself during the summertime in the vacation church schools and during the rest of the year in the youth programs. The Fellowship expects to achieve a high percentage of contact with all rural young people of Grant County.

The population, with the exception of the two urban centers, is diminishing. More than sixty per cent of the out-of-high-school-aged young people leave Grant County. The Fellowship is contemplating a program by which opportunities for farming and the establishment of business will be presented to challenge young people. To make Grant County a more attractive place in which to earn a living and raise a family is a new goal for the Fellowship. A committee will be put into operation to bring together jobs and young people, farms and those who desire to operate them.

Because the people in the participating churches have been isolated from each other for so many years, a new program of publicity is being developed. By the use of direct mail as well as county newspapers, information about the activity of the Fellowship will consistently be brought before the attention of the people.

It is too early to make a final judgment about the effectiveness of this type of larger parish. However, there are certain indications already that can be mentioned.

The pastors and executives are working together for the general welfare of the Kingdom first. Where churches need to be combined or portions of programs need to be carried out together, these things are being done.

The downward trend in membership in both the church schools and congregations has been halted, and a new and rapid upward trend can already be charted.

The same is true in regard to church finances. It is to be noted, however, that the economic situation has been much better in recent years. Moreover, the upswing financially in the Grant County Fellowship is at a much more rapid rate than that of the surrounding economic world.

Thus, we see that the interdenominational larger parish may be developed from two different points of view: the first we have described as the closely organized and integrated parish; the second, as a parish of much looser construction developed on a voluntary basis, utilizing its available leadership to promote and accomplish goals that are mutual for all the participating churches. In areas where churches are not too distant from each other and where overchurching is apparent, it is worth-while to attempt the development of a larger parish.

Chapter 11

THE DIFFICULT PARISH

IT IS NOT POSSIBLE to give a definition of the difficult parish that will fit every case; a description, however, is relatively simple. In almost every section of the country there are situations in which it becomes impractical if not impossible to carry on a normal type of church work. It may be that a small group of people is isolated by natural geographical barriers. This group is neither strong enough to maintain a formal church nor significant enough to catch the attention of the mission boards of some denomination.

Sometimes a small group of Protestant people are separated from friends by a large area occupied by non-Protestant people. Such a handful may also find it impossible to develop church work. There are large sections of the country that are so sparsely populated that the distances become too great for consistent church work. No one section of the country is predominantly given to these situations; rather, they are scattered throughout the United States. These people often feel the need for definite religious service. They find themselves missing spiritual guidance, to which they have a right. It is especially among the children and young people that these needs are apparent. Older people who have moved into the area retain the influence of earlier acquired church habits. There remains a carry-over from childhood. However, their children, born in the area where church work has not been conducted, are the ones who suffer. The real problems are: How can these people be reached? And how can such "difficult parishes" be served?

There are three possible solutions: (1) the part-time church; (2) "the church in your house," with its variations; and (3) the church on wheels.

The Part-time Church

The part-time church is to be differentiated from a multipoint parish. In a multipoint parish, a pastor's time is shared by two, three, or more churches. In a part-time church, because there are no other churches sufficiently near at hand to share the time of a pastor, the man who is chosen serves on a part-time basis. Because the church is unable to pay him a sufficient salary for full-time service, he must occupy himself at some other work in order to support his family. Thus he shares his time, not between several churches, but between a church and a job.

For many years the well-established denominations have opposed this concept. Their reasoning has been based upon the idea that a man who gives part-time service to the church and part-time to another job will have a divided allegiance. As the other work brings in more money, he is likely to spend more of his time in his secular employment. Many pastors also feel that this arrangement is haphazard and that they lose prestige in the eyes of fellow pastors under such circumstances. This feeling against a part-time ministry is reflected in the attitudes of theological students. For a number of years one of the true-false questions that the author has given to all the students in his pastoral theology course has been, "Is it ever legitimate for a pastor to work at secular employment?" Most students answer this question with an emphatic, "No!" Their answers are a reflection of the prevailing concepts among the various denominations. The arguments against this technique are based upon false premises.

Although the opposition to this concept is very strong, there have been phenomenally successful churches whose ministry has been a part-time one. The Mennonite and Amish groups do not have a paid ministry. Their pastors work at other occupations yet, upon their election as pastors, they give their services to the congregation. This has also been true among the Latter-Day Saints. The only real obstacle to this plan is a mental attitude.

By describing several examples of a part-time church with a part-time ministry, we can explain more thoroughly how this plan can best operate. Near Center Town an ethnic group of northern Europeans settled some seventy-five years ago. This group expected to develop, and hoped that other people from the same section of Europe would settle in their neighborhood. They built themselves a small one-room church. A few years later a parsonage was constructed. For twenty years resident pastors were employed. In those early years a small cash salary was paid. The rest of the pastor's income was in food, food for animals, etc. However, during this period a sociological change was taking place in the area. A large number of Roman Catholics from Europe moved into the section and began to purchase land. The Protestant group remained static in size. For a period of almost forty-five years it was not possible to employ a full-time pastor. Finally a different plan was devised. A young man was contacted who agreed to live in the parsonage to serve the people as their pastor. The people were able to contribute only approximately one third of the necessary cash income. In a little city, fourteen miles distant, he found work in a machine shop, using a skill that he had developed during the Second World War. For five years he has been serving the congregation with week-end and evening services. The people are being visited, the church services are held faithfully, a pastor once again lives in the parsonage, and a significant contribution to this small group of Protestants is being made.

Another example is to be found in an open country church situation. Because of poor land practices the population in the area diminished and the church, once flourishing, was faced with the need to close its doors permanently because no minister was available. A young man who had woodworking as his hobby offered his services to the congregation with the stipulation that he be permitted to carry on his hobby to help to finance himself and his family. Interestingly enough the hobby has developed into a second contact with members of the small church. The homes of many of the members needed remodeling. Their pastor does most of the remodeling and almost all the cabinetwork. He is being kept busy helping his people to improve their homes and also taking care of their spiritual needs.

Other examples of effective service in this speciality might be cited. One pastor who had developed electrical skills wired houses, repaired radios, and had a small appliance store while he served the people of a small congregation which would otherwise have been without the services of a minister.

Quite a number of successful examples in which the part-time pastor engaged in farming a small acreage might be cited. In some areas churches own forty and even sixty acres of land. The pastor farms this land and receives as part of his remuneration the proceeds from the land. There are other examples in which the congregation was able to rent a tract of land which the pastor worked as part of his salary.

The major danger in these arrangements is that the attention of the pastor becomes centered in his secular employment and that he neglects his own preparation as a pastor. However, this danger can safely be avoided or overcome if at the very start written agreements are made with the congregation and if the pastor from the beginning accepts this church as his real obligation. The important element is not whether the pastor makes part of his living from some source outside his church, but rather that people who would otherwise be entirely deprived of the services of a church are being contacted and served.

"The Church in Your House"

This idea is as old as the Church itself. During the period of the first century when Christianity and the Christian movement first got under way, it was necessary and customary for groups of believers to meet together in each other's homes. It may be that participants took turns in providing the place of meeting. During the early periods of persecution as well as in later centuries the same method was employed. When Christians were prevented from meeting in their church buildings, they would slip away to homes of members and hold their services in private.

In many sections of the United States, people live widely scattered from one another. For many of these families it is impossible to attend services at some central point. Distances are frequently excessive. Roads are often impassable. For thirty of forty families scattered throughout a mountainous section or in the grazing lands of the Western plains to build and maintain a church becomes a major problem for which they have not found a solution. For such people the regular denominations ought to appoint itinerant pastors whose major responsibility would be to a certain area of scattered people. This section might consist of a county or possibly two counties. The pastor would visit the people from time to time. On Sunday meetings would be arranged in the homes. One week one family would gather the nearest neighbors together and the pastor would conduct the services in that home. The next week he might be meeting in a home twenty or twenty-five miles distant, and during a third week at another location. Some denominations do carry on a somewhat similar but less concentrated ministry. In the Presbyterian Church such a pastor has been called a Sunday school missionary.

Several examples dealing with the needs of scattered families will help to clarify the necessity of developing this technique. A pastor from a well-established Midwestern church took his wife and two children on a trip through the Rocky Mountain area. As they raced along one of the paved highways of Wyoming, a monument by the side of the road attracted their attention. On the monument was the following inscription: "Lovingly dedicated to the memory of Old Blue, the best darn cow pony that ever pulled on a rope. Members of the Lazy X Ranch." The children in the family, who had never seen a real cowboy, insisted that the pastor turn into the drive that led to the ranch home. Beyond the range gate, the trail led for two and one half miles across rolling hills and through sweeping valleys. At last the car came to the end of the trail. A typical Western ranch house was built against the southern slope of a hill. The owner of the ranch came to the door of the car with a look of inquiry. The pastor had no other course but to explain the truth. They had come to see cowboys. The rancher laughed and called one of his hands to escort the children around the corral so that they might watch the cowboys at work. Then he turned his eyes of inquiry upon the pastor and asked him his business. The following conversation took place:

"I am a preacher," said the pastor. The rancher began to laugh, and replied, "Do you know that you are the first darn preacher that has been on this place in sixteen years?" The result of the conversation was an invitation to dinner. After the meal had been prepared and set out on a table on the veranda, the cowboys were called. There were two children in the family, one a boy of fifteen and the other a girl of twelve. After they had all been seated at the table, an uncomfortable pause resulted. At last the rancher looked up at the minister and said, " Well, preacher, you might as well do it." The preacher took his cue and said a table prayer. During the meal the conversation focused itself upon the lack of church contact in the entire area. The rancher explained that both his children had never been inside a church. They had had absolutely no religious instruction. He went on to tell about his own boyhood in this area. A minister used to come on horseback and spend as much as a week in their home. He would instruct the children, and on Sunday neighbors within reach would come together for a service in the home. Then he would move on to another almost inaccessible ranch home and repeat his program. This was continued from some years. After this pastor had died, no one took his place. The rancher expressed his sincere and heartfelt wish that somehow a pastor might again come to them to instruct the children and lead the families in worship.

Several years ago the author received a letter from a rancher in north central Montana. The letter described the scattered ranch homes, the isolation in wintertime, the difficulties of communications, and at the same time described the spiritual needs and religious longings of the people in the area. The rancher wanted to know whether it would be possible to assign a pastor to the area even though no church building existed. The people were willing to take care of a pastor financially. They would supply him with a jeep for summer travel and a horse when no other mode of travel was possible. He would need to develop a program of religious services from home to home. These two examples show the need for the re-establishment of the church in the home. If the rural people of our own country are to be reached by the church, serious consideration must be given to the many thousands who are scattered and far distant from any regularly organized church program.

The Church on Wheels

A number of denominations and faith groups have experimented with the church on wheels. In a section of the country where Protestantism is exceedingly scattered, some method of contact for the people needs to be maintained. The State of Utah has been used as an example. The ministry might well be known as a trailer ministry. There are two distinct concepts that should be explained. In the first, a pastor is appointed to a large area. Instead of a manse in which to live, the denomination provides him with a trailer. Thus, he is able to move his place of habitation from section to section as he changes his place of ministration. He may spend six weeks in one village area, gathering together Protestants of every denomination who are without a church home. During this time he conducts courses in Christian education, revival meetings, and regular worship services. The meeting places may be varied. Frequently some church no longer used is available. Sometimes a hall can be rented. At other times it is necessary to meet in homes. He then moves on to another section and repeats this function. In the course of a year, he may be able to serve a dozen communities. There are some very evident objections to this plan. As the minister moves from one community to another, contacts with the first area are lost. Many of the spiritual advances that have been made disappear when the pastor leaves. When he returns to the first place of service after almost a year's absence, his work must be begun all over again. On the other hand, there are some values in this process that cannot be ignored. Leadership can be established within each small group. This leadership then becomes responsible for carrying on the religious work during the periods in which the pastor is serving another area. The success of this technique is entirely dependent upon the development of such local leadership. A consecrated layman can do much to conserve the advances made while the pastor is absent.

The second concept centers itself around a trailer chapel. Special trailers have been constructed in which a small chapel with a seating capacity of ten to twenty people has been arranged. This trailer can be converted at night into living quarters for the pastor. The Roman Catholic Church used this technique in the Kentucky and Tennessee area. Thus the Church was able to bring its services to its widely scattered constituency.

Years ago the American Baptist Convention had several chapel cars. These were large railroad cars which provided living quarters for the pastor and his helper and also contained a small chapel with a seating capacity for as many as forty people. These chapel cars toured the plains states and the Pacific Northwest. As a community was found that had no adequate services, a chapel car was sent by railroad into the area and placed upon a siding. The pastor would conduct his services both during the week and on the Sabbath. A real need was met through this method.

In most of the population centers churches with their buildings have since been developed. Now the need does not lie in the population centers any longer. The need today is to be found in the small crossroads communities that are far from railroads and even isolated from trunk highways. Tourists who are willing to leave the well-marked highways will frequently find such small neighborhoods and communities. Many of these are without church services. The trailer church is especially designed to meet these needs. More men who are willing to provide this type of ministry are needed.

Although this chapter has been called "The Difficult Parish," there actually are few things that are too difficult to accomplish. A fresh approach with ingenious planning, a willingness to consecrate self, a feeling of challenge on the part of young people to rendering worth-while service to people in need — these are ingredients that help to conquer the seemingly impossible.

Thus for almost every need a solution can be found, and the rural people in every section of the United States, whether in a well-populated area or in an almost inaccessible isolated area, may have the services of the church.

Chapter 12

FINANCING THE RURAL CHURCH

ONE OF THE MOST FREQUENT REASONS given for the ineffectiveness of the town and country church is that of inadequate finances. Apparently most people agree that the lack of finances limits the effectiveness of any program that the rural church might carry out. First of all they point out that the rural church is often plagued by inadequately trained leaders and by such as have failed elsewhere. They predicate this statement upon lack of adequate finances. Larger salaries will attract better leaders. More finances will make possible more adequate properties, which again will attract better leaders. Almost all reasons that are given to explain the decline of the influence of the rural church eventually find their roots in an inadequate program of finance.

To help to solve this matter of finance, most denominations have gone into a progressive program of subsidies or mission aid. Some denominations have developed a very excellent program of aid to needy rural churches. However, after they have provided subsidies for years, the basic difficulties of the rural church have not been solved. In many cases subsidies have acted as deterrents to success rather than as aids. Churches that received mission aid year after year developed a false concept of stewardship. Instead of attempting to help themselves, they became so dependent upon outside financial assistance that they imagined it to be the duty of the denomination to help them and that it was their prerogative to request this assistance.

On the other hand there are many rural churches that have faced this temptation and have conquered it. Having studied their own needs and situations, they have developed progressive programs of finance that have made them self-supporting.

Recently a rural church of 123 members was called to the author's attention. This small group of people had met a budget of $9,000 for congregational expenses and $5,000 for mission and benevolence purposes: a total of $14,000. A few years before this church had been unable to provide itself with a full-time ministry. This amazing progress had been achieved through self-study and the development of a realistic stewardship program.

The question that is frequently asked by rural churches is, How can the necessary budget be raised? In this chapter a few successful financial techniques are presented.

A Stewardship Program

As has just been mentioned in this chapter, rural churches have been so frequently subsidized by denominational boards that they have lost sight of their real potential of giving. A pastor needs to lead such a church in a carefully planned program of self-study in its relationship toward the obligation of good stewardship. Frank discussions need to be carried on in informal groups. In the leadership training classes, the place of stewardship should be prominently examined. Boys and girls in the church school and confirmation classes need to be informed that part of the Christian heritage is consecrated stewardship. The pastor's preaching should again and again emphasize the responsibility of stewardship for all of life. This is a program of information that is primary to any particular plan of fund-raising. If the people do not have a heart for stewardship, no technique can ever succeed. If, however, the people understand and appreciate the privilege of good stewardship, any well-developed technique of fund-raising will bear rewarding fruits.

The Every Member Canvass

It is not necessary to explain the methods of developing an every member canvass. Thus far in the consciousness of the Christian Church, the most effective fund-raising technique has been the every member canvass. Denominations have carefully developed this plan and are ready to supply all necessary materials to the local church for conducting such a campaign.

The Lord's Portion Plan (also known as the Lord's Acre Plan)

No matter how well-planned the every member canvass is, there are many town and country churches that are hampered in their financing by a limited membership. If such churches desire to carry on a well-rounded program, some additional method of fund-raising must be employed. Some rural churches may have sufficient money to carry on the regular program of the church. However, if property improvement becomes necessary or some emergency arises, the membership is unable to meet the additional financial drain. In either case, the Lord's Portion Plan has been exceedingly successful.

Under this plan farmers set aside a certain portion of their produce which is in addition to their regular contribution to the church. Examples are here cited:

1. One farmer may set aside a certain number of rows of corn.
2. Another farmer may cultivate a portion of land that has thus far been idle and plant it to potatoes.
3. A third person may raise a pig or a calf as his portion.
4. Sunday evening's eggs might be set aside.
5. Young people might raise a setting of chickens, a turkey, a goose, or some ducks.

People in the village may also have opportunity to participate in the program:

1. One storekeeper joined forces with a farmer. The storekeeper bought two calves. The farmer fed and cared for them. When these were ready for market, the contribution was a joint one between the storekeeper and the farmer.
2. Other members of the church living in the village donated their services in labor when work needed to be done at the church.
3. A hardware merchant designated 5 per cent of a certain Saturday's total sales.
4. Women made certain articles of fancywork.

Many other ideas can be put to work in this Lord's Portion Plan. Usually a day is set when all these gifts are sold. Frequently this day is in the fall and known as the harvest festival. Various techniques have been employed on this day. The farm produce and all gifts have been brought together at a central place. An auction sale, which has been well advertised, is then held. The total proceeds are assigned to the work of the church. Pictures of the festival can be used in another year for wider publicity.

The results of the Lord's Portion Plan are twofold. First, it deepens the consecration of good stewardship for all who participate in it. Whenever people work with the land or their animals or donate some of their labor, they are reminded of their responsibility as good stewards. Secondly, the financial returns are usually beyond expectation. The author knows of churches that have raised from $1,500 to $7,000 by this technique. As a result many churches that carried on a very limited program were able to expand their plans and acquire strong leadership. A danger that must carefully be avoided is one that may tempt the participants in the Lord's Portion Plan to withdraw their personal pledges and contributions in favor of the Lord's Portion Plan of financing. Each member must continue his own personal good stewardship in addition to the program of the Lord's Portion.

Pastor Dumont Clarke, director of the Religious Department of the Farmers Federation at Asheville, North Carolina, has done more to explain, promote, and organize the Lord's Acre Plan than anyone else. For twenty-three years he has been an authority in its use. In the February, 1949, edition of the Lord's Acre supplement to *The Farmers Federation News,* he explained the Lord's Acre Plan, with its benefits, as follows:

"The Lord's Acre plan is that each member of the country church and all who receive the benefits of the church shall set aside, and dedicate to the Lord, some worthy portion of a farm crop or of the farm stock, raise the produce, sell it, and give the cash proceeds to the church. It is the only way that many can give. For those who are already making substantial cash gifts this plan is intended to be supplementary. The standard for the Lord's Acre, or the Lord's Acre proceeds together with the weekly cash gift, is the tithe. Group projects as well as individual projects may be carried out.

1. "It helps to enlist all ages in sacrificial Christian work.

"The Bible teaches that it is the duty of each and all to work for the Kingdom of God. 'Be ye . . . always abounding in the work of the Lord.' I Cor. 15:58. The working church, as well as the worshiping church, is necessary for the Christian development of the individual and of the community. The Lord's Acre Plan unites young and old in a fellowship of Christian work and offers an approach to many people outside the Church as an aid to evangelism.

2. "It brings financial support for special needs and advances.

"This practical plan, which supplements the system of weekly cash contributions, brings new and substantial financial returns. It develops hitherto unused resources both in the membership of the church and among others who attend the church. As experience shows, it works!

3. "It deepens the recognition that God is the source of all life and growth, and that man should be a good steward of the soil and of its produce.

"The Lord's Acre Plan, in a most effective way, gives daily expression to great Bible teachings: 'The earth is the Lord's, and the fulness thereof.' Ps. 24:1. 'Be ye doers of the word, and not hearers only.' James 1:22. 'Bring ye all the tithes into the storehouse.' Mal. 3:10.

4. "It trains the children and many older people in Christian stewardship.

"The Lord's Acre Plan is an ideal means of stewardship training, especially for children. Instead of the parents' putting church contributions into their children's hands, the work for God with field or animal projects teaches children to serve; it develops their ability, and their character is strengthened by working for the Master and the Church he established. It gives to each worker the spiritual satisfaction of doing a worthy part for the support of the church. On the other hand, what a spiritual deprivation — and financial loss to the church — when boys and girls are not trained to work for their contributions!

5. "It serves to gain the co-operation of many agencies for building Christian communities.

"The increasing adoption of the Lord's Acre Plan by the leaders of Future Farmers and the 4-H club promises to bring the life of the church much more effectively into the life of the community in a most beneficial relationship. Spiritual zest along with scientific instruction will be given for improving the standards of farming, and greater interest in the church will result from working for the church.

6. "It helps to raise up leadership for the Kingdom of God.

"Much of the church program for raising up Christian leadership, such as preaching and Bible school teaching, chiefly conveys spiritual *impression*. More *expression* in purposeful activity of these spiritual impressions is imperatively needed. The Lord's Acre Plan provides an expression in creative work for the membership as a whole that tends to develop leadership, and that contributes helpfully to every phase of church life."

A variation of the Lord's Portion Plan has also proved itself successful. A church located in a town surrounded by ranching country embarked on this program. The men in the town purchased a total of sixty calves. These calves were placed under the supervision of the ranchers who were affiliated with the church. For two years they were cared for by the ranchers and allowed to range with the other cattle. At the end of that time they were gathered together and sold. The income made possible the completion of a Christian education building which was badly needed by the local church and which up to that time had not been possible because of limited finances.

The Church Farm

In some areas it is practical for the church to rent an acreage, sixty or eighty acres lying within the church community. The official board of the local church must negotiate according to best business practices with the owner of the land for the purpose of acquiring it on a rental basis as the church farm. This farm is then to be cropped on a co-operative basis. People in the village supply the labor, the farmers lend their machinery, seed must be purchased by the church and the cost taken from the final proceeds. At the end of the season, the harvest is gathered in and sold. After rent and seed have been paid for, the proceeds are turned over to the church. Under this plan several precautions should be pointed out. A disproportionate part of the responsibility for labor frequently falls upon the shoulders of a few. The committee in charge of the farming enterprise should be exceedingly careful to divide the responsibility and the labor with equity among the participating members. Another precaution that needs to be stated deals with the whole matter of soil conservation. Frequently when a group of men farm a piece of land in common, the personal attitude and responsibility toward the land itself is lost. The result often is poor soil stewardship. Because the church is always in a position of example it is doubly important that a church farm should show every evidence of careful planning and good soil stewardship.

The Youth Budget Plan

The youth budget is not a new idea in helping to finance churches. It has been practiced on a regularly planned basis for ten years. It needs, however, to receive special attention because of its important contribution to the total life of the church. This contribution is especially significant when examined over a long period of use. In this plan all the young people in a church from three years of age through twenty-one are contacted by other young people. Those who are very young in years need the help of parents in making decisions.

In past years, especially in the rural church, families have made one pledge to the church. This has been based upon the concept that in the farming enterprise there is only one income per family. All members of the family are responsible for producing this income. Consequently one total pledge is made in the name of the entire family. This concept met the needs of our older agrarian society. Changes have been rapid in this society. In many cases members of the family have separate sources of income. Children also have an allowance and frequently a small earned income.

The habits that are formulated in early youth remain most consistently with the adult throughout his life. If habits of giving are established early, they remain with the child when he becomes an adult. It is also true that education carried on during the years of youth is most effective. "Train up a child in the way he should go, and when he is old he will not depart from it" (Prov. 22:6). The youth budget has two general major benefits: the one in its relationship to the young people, and the other in its relationship to the church.

The purpose of the plan in relationship to the young people is to develop in them Christian character and the correct concepts toward service and stewardship. Young people are anxious to feel that they are filling a needed part in the program of any of the institutions with which they are connected. The fierce loyalty of boys and girls toward their high schools is an example of this truth. These young people realize that they are exceedingly essential to the welfare of the school. Whether they participate in the drama organizations or the athletic contests or any of the other activities of the school, loyalty is assured. They know that these activities could not be continued without them.

For too many years we have kept from our young people a real sense of participation in their responsibility toward the church. Since they had no important part in its support, they felt no comparative sense of loyalty. In the development of the youth budget, their loyalty is strengthened and they feel more certain that the church belongs to them as well as to their elders.

Some of the particular purposes of the youth budget as they relate to the young people themselves are:

1. Education. When the budget of the church is presented to young people and the whole program of stewardship is explained, a process of education takes place. The young people who frequently have felt no responsibility toward the finances of the church begin to understand the need for everyone to assume his own share of the total need of the church.

2. Stewardship. Although the program of stewardship has always been rated of great importance in the Christian Church, the people themselves have interpreted it too often as merely a portion of their financial overflow. They have not felt that their financial responsibility toward the church should be a segment of their total personal income. The Youth Budget Plan has helped young people to adopt an intelligent attitude toward stewardship.

3. Democracy. The Youth Budget Plan is administered not by adults but by the young people themselves. After they have studied the needs of their church and have decided what portion is their responsibility, the budget plan makes it possible for them to present

these needs to other young people. Thus the process of democracy may be strengthened.

4. Dedication. Often the giving of both adults and young people has been haphazard. In the case of a planned program which has been approved by the group itself, both personal and group dedication to it are a usual result. This is true with youth budget planning. Young people consecrate and dedicate themselves to the larger Christian program which is made possible by their personal contributions.

The purpose of the plan in relationship to the church is also important. Year after year in those churches where the Youth Budget Plan has been adopted, an increasingly large sum of money comes from the young people. The immediate aid that the local church received from these monies is important. However, much more important is the eventual assistance that comes to the church from young people growing into adulthood. The proportion of giving to income by young people growing into adulthood who have been raised with the Youth Budget Plan is comparably much higher than in the case of those who never contribute on a systematic basis until they have established families of their own.

In inaugurating the Youth Budget Plan in the rural church the following steps should be taken:

1. As has been pointed out frequently, whenever a new program is introduced to any organization, the first step is that of good publicity and education. The pastor should call together a number of young people, with a Sunday school teacher, an official board member, and several parents. A careful and thoroughgoing discussion about the youth budget and how it has worked in many contemporary situations should then be conducted. The pastor must be prepared to answer the many questions that will arise during the period of discussion. Sometimes it is helpful to call in the pastor of some neighboring church where the youth budget has been adopted, or, better still, one of the young people, to explain the plan as it has functioned in his church. There are also moving pictures available which are helpful in introducing the plan.

2. After this preliminary discussion, and after the approval of

the official church board has been obtained, a committee to carry on the campaign should be set up. This committee should have an adult adviser, preferably one of the trustees of the church. Members of the committee will then meet to set up a budget within the total budget of the church. The committee not only will attempt in this program to cover the items of expense that normally arise in the conducting of Sunday school and youth programs, but also will make an effort to include additional items such as a share of the congregation's expense and a share of benevolence.

3. The young people should next have an opportunity to approve the budget set up by their committee. A problem arises that is centered around the ages of the young people. For the normal youth organizations to accept the budget would not be difficult. The problem lies with the Sunday school. Youngsters of kindergarten and primary ages do not comprehend the significance of budget-making. Consequently the approval of the Sunday school may best be sought through its teachers and officers. Another possible suggestion would be for the classes from nine years of age upward to have the budget presented to them.

4. The committee next prepares and conducts the every youth canvass. Teams of three can best be sent out to call upon the young people connected with the church. These teams will contact the families of children who are very young in age. It is important to point out that a child receiving an allowance of 25 cents a week should be permitted to make his pledge himself. He will, however, need careful guidance. Sometimes his enthusiasm will lead him to assign too large a portion of his allowance to the canvass. Both the parents and the committee should give guidance in this matter.

5. After the drive has been completed, the teams and the committee gather to make an accurate accounting of the canvass. They will then turn the results over to the official board of the church. Members of the official board will do well to congratulate the young people upon their work.

Miscellaneous Techniques

Church magazines suggest various methods of finance to their readers. Certain companies, especially those who have extracts for sale, try to interest church groups in the sale of their products. Many church organizations have sold a hundred bottles of vanilla and received a coffee maker in return. Other organizations have sold magazines. Some companies have provided all the necessary materials to put on a pancake supper in the church for the privilege of advertising their products. The rural church should be very careful in choosing miscellaneous ways of financing. Although ethically there may be no objection to the utilization of these commercial techniques, they do not do much good so far as the concept of stewardship is concerned in the Christian Church.

Some rural churches that are situated in villages or small towns have utilized a technique which at best may be questioned in its ethics. Once a week or once a month they have held a major church supper for the sole purpose of raising funds rather than strengthening fellowship and brotherhood. Some time ago the author drove through a small town and stopped at a restaurant for supper. He was the only customer in the place. In conversation with the proprietor he learned that each week the local churches took turns in serving suppers to help to finance their organization. On these days the restaurant had no local business whatsoever. The proprietor pointed out that he was the one who was making the major contribution to these churches because on that evening they had taken his source of income from him. The ethics of such a procedure should be questioned and rural churches ought never to participate in this type of effort.

Among some Protestant as well as Roman Catholic churches bingo games have been conducted. Any kind of gaming device for the players' gain that includes the spirit of gambling must be entirely avoided in the financing of the rural church. The church must always keep its financial program on the highest plane of consecrated stewardship.

Chapter 13

THE RURAL CHURCH BUILDING

At the present time, because of existing conditions and our machine age, the building that houses the church plays a much more significant part in the total program than at any prior time. In the past the rural church had very few subordinate organizations. The congregation met on Sunday for corporate worship and for instruction in the Christian religion. Because there were few supporting organizations, the building was used only one day. Consequently the earlier buildings in town and country areas were very simple. The one-room structure with or without a basement was the general rule. After some years the need to expand facilities seemed essential. The decision then had to be made whether the building already constructed could be made adequate with an addition or whether an entirely new structure was called for. In most cases a new building was erected. In rural areas of the Middle West and West, this second wave of building took place from 1910 to 1929. These buildings included a place of worship, a full basement with a furnace, and possibly a kitchen and dining room and a number of Sunday school rooms on the same level with the worship room. These buildings were erected just at the beginning of a much-expanded concept of church work.

Although the congregations have not grown larger numerically, the number of meetings has risen considerably and the uses to which the building is put have increased remarkably. Although the cost of construction at the present time is excessive, many rural congregations are facing the problem again. Most of their buildings were soundly constructed and in many cases it would seem to be a waste of effort and money to tear them down and build entirely new structures. Consequently these congregations are face to face with a problem of remodeling their churches or adding rooms to their buildings so that the needs of the present congregation can be more nearly met.

It is definitely not the purpose of this chapter to suggest floor plans or blueprints for rural congregations to follow. It is the purpose of this chapter, however, to point out the techniques that local congregations should use in approaching the whole program of building.

The Building Committee

Whether a church faces the need to build or not, it should, nevertheless, have a building committee. There are always needs that must be met in regard to the structure. Sometimes a new roof is essential, windows must be releaded, a heating plant rebuilt, the electrical wiring of the church examined, etc. All these functions should be placed in the hands of a permanent building committee. Then when the time comes that major structural changes must be made or more room must be supplied, a committee will already be empowered to study those needs and to suggest a procedure to the congregation. The building committee that faces major construction should approach the problem with exceeding care. Certain preliminary steps ought to be taken before the advice of an architect is sought.

1. The first question that must be answered is, Just why do we need a major building program? The committee should study the background out of which this need has arisen. It should also study the future of the community both as to population and services. Because the experiences of the past and the needs of the present cannot alone determine the kind of changes that must be made, the requirements of a foreseeable future must also be considered. After the committee has made this study and has met at frequent intervals to put on paper the results of the study, the next step should be taken.

2. Educating the congregation. Many building programs have been wrecked because the congregation was not consulted at the very earliest point in the planning. This does not presuppose that

the congregation will approve any program of extensive building. It merely assures the members of the church that no committee is trying to sell them a bill of goods with which they have not been made familiar from the very start. The methods of publicity are the same as are used to inform the congregation about other items of interest. If there is a monthly newssheet, the needs can be presented in it. Pastoral letters may be employed. If the Sunday school is inadequately housed, a written statement from the officers and teachers of the Sunday school should be sent into every home. Much general discussion concerning building needs should carefully be directed in each organization that uses the facilities of the church. After a period of publicity and after the various organizations have had an opportunity to express their general needs to the building committee, the next step seems natural.

3. An architect should be consulted. Most readers can call to mind many churches that have been remodeled without consulting an experienced architect. The results have frequently been monstrosities of architecture. In almost every case an architect can lead a congregation out of frequent pitfalls in building that do not seem apparent to the laymen. This is not only true with a job of reconstruction; it is also true when an entirely new building is to be erected. Rural church plans are available from the several denominational boards. Blueprints can be obtained, but in spite of these services it still remains the best procedure to consult an architect and to hire him when building plans have progressed sufficiently.

4. The next procedure is to win the approval in general of the congregation itself. It is impossible at this time to indicate the extent of remodeling and rebuilding or its cost. The congregation should, therefore, permit the building committee to draw up specific plans both of building and of finance which are to be submitted to the congregation for adoption at a later date.

5. The committee is now ready to proceed specifically. Immediately a group of subcommittees must be appointed. Each organization using the church facilities should have its own representative or committee which will report to the building committee. From the congregation three major committees should be appointed: (1) worship, (2) music, and (3) congregational participation. It will be the

duty of these committees to suggest ideas in each of their specific fields. The worship committee will study whether a pulpit-centered church or an open chancel should be used. It will also suggest worship aids. The music committee will study the problem of organ and choir location and matters pertaining to these. The congregation participation committee will study the seating of the congregation, facilities for taking care of wraps, possibility of a mothers' room, etc.

Each organization will receive instruction to hand in two plans covering its needs. The one plan will be the minimum requirement, the other the maximum desirable. For example, the women's organization will suggest the kind of facilities that would be most desirable to carry on its work. These will deal with kitchen, dining facilities, meeting room, lounges, etc. They will also prepare a plan that they feel would be the absolute minimum under which the organization can function well. The young people will hand in a similar plan, as will the Sunday school, scouts, 4-H clubs, or any other organizations affiliated with the church. While this planning is being developed by the organizations, the building committee will appoint a committee on financing.

6. The committee on finance always has a major problem to face. To set up the approximate cost of reconstruction or of building an entirely new church is dependent upon many variables. The committee will need to investigate local costs of both material and labor. Other congregations that have completed a program may be visited and the officers interviewed for advice. After all the suggestions of the various study committees have been brought together, the committee on finance will be ready to develop its suggestions. The architect will carefully examine all suggested ideas and will make several tentative plans from which costs can be estimated. After these have been estimated the building committee will need to add at least ten per cent to the total before a realistic figure can be presented to the congregation.

7. A special congregational meeting for the purpose of discussing and either adopting or rejecting plans will then be called. At this time the building committee will present a condensed schedule of all suggestions made by the church's organizations. If it is possible for the architect to be present, he will be called upon to explain the

program of building and to answer questions concerning structure.

The finance committee will propose several plans of financing the venture. In many cases a three-year program of contributions has been found most satisfactory.

8. The congregation, having had all plans carefully presented, will make its decision relative to building. If the vote favors building, the financial committee will be empowered immediately to make a drive for funds. If adequate funds are not pledged, the congregation will need to meet either to authorize an additional drive or to curtail the building program. On the other hand, when sufficient funds have been pledged, the plans for construction may proceed. It is seldom wise when building or reconstructing a church to proceed unless at least fifty per cent of the funds are in hand. In a rural church the ability to contribute is directly related to weather, crops, and markets. Frequently these cause such fluctuations in the finances of the people that a serious situation might arise if a church proceeds to build with only one third of the cash in hand. This does not mean that a congregation should proceed if fifty per cent of the needed funds are pledged. A rural church should seldom go into debt beyond twenty-five per cent of the total cost of construction (this debt is to be considered as that which is beyond the amount of money pledged by constituent members plus the cash on hand).

Chapter 14

THE FORWARD LOOK

To INDICATE that rural work is made up of problems almost too difficult to solve would be inaccurate. In the development of a progressive church program the problems and difficulties are bound to become apparent and these must be approached with determination and courage. Much of this book has been written in order that tools and techniques might be presented that would, with proper leadership and direction, go far in the solution of the problems.

There is also a real and fascinating challenge for the rural leader in the rural church. This challenge is large enough for the most able; it is intriguing enough for the best scholar; it is broad enough for the most ambitious.

The challenge to the rural worker is one to make the rural church the conservator of American family life. In almost every section of our culture the family as a unit has been assailed directly or indirectly. Its unity has progressively been attacked by diversified interests. Among rural people the leadership of the church now has a new opportunity to emphasize the values in family living. Beginning with the family altar the rural people can rediscover the joy of unit worship. In the tasks of the day, because most families labor together, the church can reinterpret the obligation of work and the holiness of labor.

The rural church can again become the initiator of community action. All too often there is no leadership within the community by which action can be instituted. The church is again in a position to do so. Whether the need is for a community calendar, a new county hospital, recreational facilities, or a highway safety campaign, the church with its leadership should become the initiator of the program. It is concerned not only with man's spiritual welfare, but also with his social and community relationships.

The rural church can and should interpret the community mores. It ought to become the conscience of community. For a number of years the schools took this place, but since the schools are gradually developing into larger units, and are being consolidated in areas too distant from the local communities to be effective, the rural church ought again to become the conscience. Pastors and lay leaders alike may join together to introduce the good, to encourage the worthwhile, and to give direction to all positive action. On the other hand the leadership of the rural church may also frown upon and bring pressure against those practices within the community that destroy and tear down family, home, and community oneness.

The rural church, with intelligent leadership using careful methods for the development of constructive plans, can become the very heart of its community. This does not mean that the church or its leaders should ever dictate a policy or a program to the people of the community. It does, however, mean that the church, using its best methods, shall constantly guide, counsel, and co-operate with other institutions that are functioning for the good of the community. This means that the leaders of the church can best express their Christian faith through positive community action which will affect both themselves and their neighbors.

The rural community, whether large or small, does bring its influence to bear upon the larger community, namely, the entire nation. It is important what the local pastor does, because through the lives of people touched by his program, his influence is felt in every walk of life.

The rural community at Cross Roads is not only important to itself, and to its country; it is also important in its relationship to the world. We, as rural people, cannot escape our responsibility to the world as a whole even though we seek to do so.

More than seventy per cent of the total population of our world is rural. Because the balance of population in the United States has become favorable to the urban situation, many church leaders have lost sight of the more extensive world outlook. We have recognized in our population situations that the United States no longer exists as an isolated entity. Increasingly we have become aware of our world relationship and our responsibility. What occurs to people in northern Europe affects us. The future of the millions in Pakistan is our business. How Africa's native people develop their civilizations will bring influence to bear in the future upon our homes and interrelationships. Because the Christian religion is the one surviving force that has within it the power to bring brotherhood to all mankind upon the earth, the relationship of our Christian Church in America will be profoundly influenced by rural concepts for centuries to come. Just because our farm population has diminished today is not a time for us to take our attention from the rural church. Many denominations are inclined to do so. They excuse themselves for neglecting the rural church on the basis that our American population living in continental climates is inclined to shift to the more moderate climates of the southwest, the southeast, and the far west. Denominational leaders therefore assume that the influence of rural work will continue to diminish because numerically the population of the United States is decreasing in rural areas.

A trend in the opposite direction, however, has become apparent, particularly in the schools of our land. Nationals from predominantly rural countries are coming to our seminaries for training. They are especially interested in the careful acquisition of rural techniques and information. Recognizing that the major needs of their own native country are predominantly in the rural fields, they come to America for help. Therefore from the world point of view it behooves us to increase our experience in rural work and to develop techniques by which the rural people of the world can best be contacted for Christ and the Church.

In our town and country areas the need for a continued emphasis on the rural church will remain almost constant. Students in population and population trends are convinced that our rural population has come to the point where it soon will meet a level beyond which it is not likely to drop. They also are agreed that county seat towns and cities of 2,500 population and upward will draw families to the surrounding areas. They also predict that the rural nonfarm population will continue to increase. Thus the rural church may need to shift some of its emphasis from the rural farm people to the rural nonfarm population. The general work of the rural church will continue unabated. With a better-trained leadership in the rural church the problem of the unreached which has developed especially in town and country areas will be solved.

Economically, rural America has advanced with great strides during the past score of years. From the economically depressed period of the early thirties to the advanced economic position of the fifties has been a long step. As these rural people develop in their sense of Christian stewardship, their churches and other institutions will also expand and become more efficient. A better leadership and more adequate equipment will be acquired.

In years past, when the economy of America was predominantly agrarian, rural pastors produced major contributions to literature and devotional materials. As our population became more urban-centered, and the emphasis of church work was shifted away from rural areas, the better-trained pastors moved to the cities. As a result, most of the literary contribution made by pastors during the past twenty-five years came from the city. The leadership of the present rural church should once again recapture a part of this field.

The rural church today holds out a real challenge for consecrated service and dedicated lives to young men who wish to make a career of serving town and country people.

BIBLIOGRAPHY

BOOKS

Rural Life and the Church, by David E. Lindstrom. The Garrard Press, 1948.

Rural Sociology, by Lowry Nelson. American Book Co., 1948.

A Study of Rural Society, by John H. Kolb and Edmund de S. Brunner. The Riverside Press, 1952 (fourth edition).

In these three books the leader for rural life will find the kind of data that will introduce him to both the town and country people, with the problems and the trends that affect their lives. It will explain the institutions and forces at work in rural America.

The Christian Mission Among Rural People. The Foreign Missions Conference of North America, 1949.

The Church in Our Town, by Rockwell C. Smith. Abingdon-Cokesbury Press, 1950.

Manual for Town and Country Churches, by Alice Maloney and Henry Randolph. Board of National Missions, Presbyterian Church, U.S.A., 1948.

Rural Prospect, by Mark Rich. Friendship Press, 1950.

Rural Synthesis, by Martin Thornton. Skeffington & Son, Ltd., London, 1948.

These five books deal directly with the work of the rural church, its techniques, its prospects, and its philosophy.

BULLETINS AND PAMPHLETS

A Checksheet for Rural Churches. Presbyterian Rural Fellowship, 156 Fifth Avenue, New York. (In process of being revised.)

The Christian Rural Fellowship Bulletins, Numbers 1 to 180. The Christian Rural Fellowship, 156 Fifth Avenue, New York.

These bulletins are an entire library of rural church information; they are a must in every rural leader's library.

Tomorrow's Community, by W. H. Stacy. Iowa State College, 1953 (third edition).

These bulletins are valuable in checking the program of the local church for effectiveness. *Tomorrow's Community* also includes check sheets for other institutions of the rural community.

MISCELLANEOUS

Cooperative Churches, by Ralph A. Felton. Madison, New Jersey, 1947.

The Cooperative Parish, by Alfred Behrer. Department of Rural Church, University of Dubuque, 1948.

The Larger Parish: An Effective Organization for Rural Churches, by Mark Rich, Extension Bulletin No. 408. College of Agriculture, Cornell University, 1939.

Study of Grant County, Wisconsin. Department of Rural Church, University of Dubuque, 1952.

These papers will be especially helpful in developing larger or co-operative parishes. The first three give directions in the actual development of such parishes. The fourth explains how the larger parish may study its community.